Poems and Ballads of Heinrich Heine

HEINRICH HEINE

New York 1881

TABLE OF CONTENTS

HEINRICH HEINE
EARLY POEMS
HOMEWARD BOUND 1823 TO 1824
SONGS TO SERAPHINE
TO ANGELIQUE
SPRING FESTIVAL
CHILDE HAROLD
THE ASRA
HELENA
SONG
THE NORTH SEA 1825 TO 1826
FIRST CYCLUS
SECOND CYCLUS

HEINRICH HEINE

BIOGRAPHICAL SKETCH

Harry Heine, as he was originally named, was born in Düsseldorf on the Rhine, December 13th, 1799. His father was a well-to-do Jewish merchant; and his mother, the daughter of the famous physician and Aulic Counlor Von Geldern, was, according to her son, a "femme distinguée." His early childhood fell in the days of the occupation of Düsseldorf by the French revolutionary troops; and, in the opinion of his biographer Strodtmann, the influence of the French rule, thus brought directly to bear upon the formation of his character, can scarcely be exaggerated. His education was begun at the Franciscan monastery of the Jesuits at Düsseldorf, where the teachers were mostly French priests; and his religious instruction was at the same time carried on in a private Jewish school. His principal companions were Jewish children, and he was brought up with a rigid adherence to the Hebrew faith. Thus in the very seed-time of his mental development were simultaneously sown the germs of that Gallic liveliness and mobility which pre-eminently distinguish him among German authors, and also of his ineradicable sympathy with things Jewish, and his inveterate antagonism to the principles and results of Christianity.
As the medical profession was in those days the only one open to Jews in Germany, the boy Heine was destined for a commercial career; and in 1815 his father took him to Frankfort to establish him in a banking-house. But a brief trial proved that he was utterly unsuited to the situation, and after two months he was back again in Düsseldorf. Three years later he went to Hamburg, and made another attempt to adopt a mercantile pursuit under

the auspices of his uncle, the wealthy banker Solomon Heine. The millionaire, however, was very soon convinced that the "fool of a boy" would never be fit for a counting-house, and declared himself willing to furnish his nephew with the means for a three years, course at the university, in order to obtain a doctor's degree and practice law in Hamburg. It was well-known that this would necessitate Harry's adoption of Christianity; but his proselytism did not strike those whom it most nearly concerned in the same way as it has impressed the world. So far from this being the case, he wrote in 1823 to his friend Moser: "Here the question of baptism enters; none of my family is opposed to it except myself; but this myself is of a peculiar nature. With my mode of thinking, you can imagine that the mere act of baptism is indifferent to me; that even symbolically I do not consider it of any importance, and that I shall only dedicate myself more entirely to upholding the rights of my unhappy brethren. But, nevertheless, I find it beneath my dignity and a taint upon my honor, to allow myself to be baptized in order to hold office in Prussia. I understand very well the Psalmist's words: 'Good God, give me my daily bread, that I may not blaspheme thy name!'"

The uncle's offer was accepted. In 1819 Harry Heine entered the university of Bonn. During his stay in Hamburg began his unrequited passion for a cousin who lived in that city a passion which inspired a large portion of his poetry, and indeed gave the keynote to his whole tone and spirit. He sings so many different versions of the same story of disappointment, that it is impossible to ascertain, with all his frank and passionate confidences, the true course of the affair. After a few months at Bonn, he removed to the university of Göttingen, which he left in 1822 for Berlin. There is no other period in the poet's career on which it is so pleasant to linger as on the two years of his residence in the Prussian capital. In his first prose work, the Letters from Berlin, published in the Rhenish-Westphalian Indicator, he has painted a vivid picture of the life and gayety of the city during its most brilliant season. "At the last rout I was particularly gay, I was so beside myself, that I really do not know why I did not walk on my head. If my most mortal enemy had crossed my path, I should have said to him, To-morrow we will kill each other, but to-night I will cordially cover you with kisses. Tu es beau, tu es charmant! Tu es l'objet de ma flamme je t'adore, ma belle! these were the words my lips repeated instinctively a hundred times; and I pressed everybody's hand, and I took off my hat gracefully to everybody, and all the men returned my civilities. Only one German youth played the boor, and railed against what he called my aping the manners of the foreign Babylon; and growled out in his old Teutonic, beer-drinking bass voice, 'At a cherman masquerade, a Cherman should speak Cherman.' Oh German youth! how thy words strike me as not only silly, but almost blasphemous at such moments, when my soul lovingly embraces the entire universe, when I would fain joyfully embrace Russians and Turks, and throw myself in tears on the breast of my brother the enslaved African!"

The doors of the most delightful, intellectual society of Germany were opened to the handsome young poet, who is described in a contemporary sketch as "beardless, blonde and pale, without any prominent feature in his face, but of so peculiar a stamp that he attracted the attention at once, and was not readily forgotten."

The daughter of Elise von Hohenhausen, the translator of Byron, has given us a charming sketch of her mother's Thursday evening receptions, which Heine regularly attended, and where he read aloud the unpublished manuscripts of his Lyrical Intermezzo, and his tragidies, Almansor and Ratcliffe. "He was obliged to submit," writes Mlle. von Hohenhausen, "to many a harsh criticism, to much severe censure; above all, he was subjected to a great deal of chaffing about his poetic sentimentality, which a few years later awakened so warm a response in the hearts of German youth. The poem, ending, Zu deinen süssen Füssen ('At thy sweet feet'), met with such laughing opposition, that he omitted it from the published edition. Opinions of his talents were various; a small minority had any suspicion of his future undisputed poetical fame. Elise von Hohenhausen, who gave him the name of the German Byron, met with many contradictions. This recognition, however, assured her an imperishable gratitude on Heine's part."

Not only his social and intellectual faculties found abundant stimulus in this bracing atmosphere, but his moral convictions were directed and strengthened by the philosophy and personal influence of Hegel, and his sympathies with his own race were aroused to enthusiastic activity by the intelligent Jews who were at that time laboring in Berlin for the advancement of their oppressed brethren. In 1819 had been formed the "Society for the Culture and Improvement of the Jews," which, though centered in Berlin, counted members all over Prussia, as well as in Vienna, Copenhagen, and New York. Heine joined it in 1822, and became one of its most influential members. In the educational establishment of the Verein, he gave for several months three hours of historical instruction a week. He frankly confessed that he, the "born enemy of all positive religions," was no enthusiast for the Hebrew faith, but he was none the less eager to proclaim himself an enthusiast for the rights of the Jews and their civil equality.

During his brief visit to Frankfort, he had had personal experience of the degrading conditions to which his people were subjected.

The contrast between his choice of residence for twenty-five years in Paris, and the tenacity with which Goethe clung to his home, is not as strongly marked as the contrast between the relative positions in Frankfort of these two men. Goethe, the grandson of the honored chief-magistrate, surrounded in his cheerful burgher-life, as Carlyle says, by "kind plenty, secure affection, manifold excitement and instruction," might well cherish golden memories of his native city. For him, the gloomy Judengasse, which he occasionally passed, where "squalid, painful Hebrews were banished to scour old clothes," was but a dark spot that only heightened the prevailing brightness of the picture. But to this wretched by-way was relegated that other beauty-enamored, artist-soul, Heine, when he dared set foot in the imperial Free Town. Here must he be locked in like a wild beast, with his miserable brethren every Sunday afternoon. And if the restrictions were a little less barbarous in other parts of Germany, yet how shall we characterize a national policy which closed to such a man as Heine every career that could give free play to his genius, and offered him the choice between money changing and medicine?

It was not till he had exhausted every means of endeavoring to secure a remission of the humiliating decree that he consented to the public act of apostasy, and was baptized in the summer of 1825 in the Lutheran parsonage of Heiligenstadt with the name of Johann Christian Heinrich. During the period of his earnest labors for Judaism, he had buried himself with fervid zeal in the lore of his race, and had conceived the idea of a prose-legend, the Rabbi of Bacharach, illustrating the persecutions of his people during the middle ages. Accounts vary as to the fate of this work; some affirm that the manuscript was destroyed in a fire at Hamburg, and others that the three chapters which the world possesses are all that were ever completed. Heine, one of the most subjective of poets, treats this theme in a purely objective manner. He does not allow himself a word of comment, much less of condemnation concerning the outrages he depicts. He paints the scene as an artist, not as the passionate fellow-sufferer and avenger that he is. But what subtle eloquence lurks in that restrained cry of horror and indignation which never breaks forth, and yet which we feel through every line, gathering itself up like thunder on the horizon for a terrific outbreak at the end!

Would that we could hear the explosion burst at last! We long for it throughout as the climax and the necessary result of the lowering electric influences of the story, and we lay aside the never-to-be completed fragment with the oppression of a nightmare. But a note of such tremendous power as Heine had struck in this romance, required for its prolonged sustention a singleness of purpose and an exaltation of belief in its efficacy and truth, which he no longer possessed after his renunciation of Judaism. He was no longer at one with himself, for no sooner was the irrevocable step taken than it was bitterly repented, not as a recantation of his principles for as such, no one who follows the development of his mind can regard it, but as an unworthy concession to tyrannic injustice. How sensitive he remained in respect to the whole question is proved most conspicuously by his refraining on all occasions from signing his Christian name, Heinrich. Even his works he caused to appear under the name of H. Heine, and was once extremely angry with his publisher for allowing by mistake the full name to be printed.

The collection of poems in prose and verse known as the Reisebilder, embraced several years of Heine's literary activity, and represent widely-varying phases of his intellectual development. We need only turn to the volumes themselves to guess how bitter an experience must have filled the gap between the buoyant stream of sunny inspiration that ripples through the Harz-Reise, and the fierce spirit of vindictive malice which prompted Heine, six years later, to conclude his third and last volume with his unseemly diatribe against Count Platen. Notwithstanding their inequalities, the Reisebilder remain one of the surest props of Heine's fame. So clear and perfect an utterance is sufficiently rare in all languages; but it becomes little short of a miracle when, as in this case, the medium of its transmission is German prose, a vehicle so bulky and unwieldy that no one before Heine had dared to enlist it in the service of airy phantasy, delicate humor and sparkling wit.

During the summer of 1830, while he was loitering at Helgoland, he was roused to feverish excitement by the news of the July Revolution. He inveighed against the nobility in a preface to a pamphlet, called Kahldorf on the Nobility, which largely increased the number of his powerful enemies. The literary censorship had long mutilated his prose writings, besides materially diminishing his legitimate income by prohibiting the sale of many of his works. He now began to fear that his personal liberty would be restricted as summarily as his literary activity; and in May, 1831, he took up his residence in Paris. He perfected himself in the French language, and by his brilliant essays on French art, German philosophy, and the Romantic School, soon acquired the reputation of one of the best prose writers of France, and the "wittiest Frenchman since Voltaire." He became deeply interested in the doctrine of St. Simonism, then at its culminating point in Paris. Its central idea of the rehabilitation of the flesh, and the sacredness of labor, found an enthusiastic champion in him who had so long denounced the impracticable spiritualism of Christianity. He, the logical clear-headed sceptic in all matters pertaining to existing systems and creeds, seems possessed with the credulity of a child in regard to every scheme of human regeneration, or shall we call it the exaltation of the Jew, for whom the Messiah has not yet arrived, but is none the less confidently and hourly expected? Embittered by repeated disappointments, by his enforced exile, by a nervous disease which had afflicted him from his youth, and was now fast gaining upon him, and by the impending shadow of actual want, Heine's tone now assumes a concentrated acridity, and his poetry acquires a reckless audacity of theme and treatment. His Neue Lieder, addressed to notorious Parisian women, were regarded as an insult to decency. In literary merit many of them vie with the best of his earlier songs; but the daring defiance of public opinion displayed in the choice of subject excluded all other criticism than that of indignation and rebuke. There is but a single ray to lighten the gathering gloom of Heine's life at this period. In a letter dated, April 11th, 1835, occurs his first mention of his liaison with the grisette Mathilde Crescence Mirat, who afterwards became his wife. This uneducated, simple-hearted, affectionate child-wife inspired in the poet, weary of intellectual strife, a love as tender and constant as it had been sudden and passionate. A variety of circumstances having combined to reduce Heine to extreme want, he had recourse to a step which has been very severely censured. He applied for and received from the French government a pension from the fund set aside for "all those who by their zeal for the cause of the Revolution had more or less compromised themselves at home or abroad." Now that the particulars of the case are so well known, it would be superfluous to add any words of justification; it can only excite our sympathy for the haughty poet doomed to drain so bitter a cup. He was pressed to take the oath of naturalization, but he had too painful experience of the renunciation of his birthright ever to consent to a repetition of his error. He would not forfeit the right to have inscribed upon his tomb-stone: "Here lies a German poet."

In 1844 his uncle Solomon died; and, as there was no stipulation in the banker's will that the yearly allowance hitherto granted to Heinrich should continue, the oldest heir Karl announced that this would altogether cease. This very cousin Karl had been nursed by Heine at the risk of his own life during the cholera-plague of 1832 in Paris. The grief and excitement caused by his kinsman's ingratitude fearfully accelerated the progress of the malady which had long been gaining upon the poet, and which proved to be a softening of the spinal cord. One eye was paralyzed, he lost the sense of taste, and complained that everything he ate was like clay. His physicians agreed that he had few weeks to live, and he felt that he was dying, little divining that the agony was to be prolonged for ten horrible years. It is unnecessary to dwell upon these years of darkness, in which Heine, shriveled to the proportions of a child, languished upon his "mattress-grave" in Paris. His patient resignation, his indomitable will, his sweetness and gayety of temper, and his unimpaired vigor and fertility of intellect, are too fresh in the memory of many living witnesses, and have been too frequently and recently described to make it needful here to enlarge upon them. In the crucial hour he proved no recreant to the convictions for which he had battled and bled during a lifetime. Of the report that his illness had materially modified his religious opinions, he has left a complete and emphatic denial. "I must expressly contradict the rumor that I have retreated to the threshold of any sort of church, or that I have reposed upon its bosom. No! My religious views and convictions have remained free from all churchdom; no belfry chime has allured me, no altar taper has dazzled me. I have trifled with no symbol, and have not utterly renounced my reason. I have forsworn nothing not even my old pagan-gods, from whom it is true I have parted, but parted in love and friendship."

"I am no longer a divine biped," he wrote. "I am no longer the freest German after Goethe, as Ruge named me in healthier days. I am no longer the great hero No. 2, who was compared with the grape-crowned Dionysius, whilst my colleague No. 1 enjoyed the title of a Grand Ducal Wlimarian Jupiter. I am no longer a joyous, somewhat corpulent Hellenist, laughing cheerfully down upon the melancholy Nazarenes. I am now a poor fatally-ill Jew, an emaciated picture of woe, an unhappy man."

Thus side by side flowed on the continuous streams of that wit and pathos which he poured forth inexhaustibly to the very end. No word of complaint or impatience ever passed his lips; on the contrary, with his old, irresistible humor, his fancy played about his own privations and sufferings, and tried to alleviate for his devoted wife and friends the pain of the heart-rending spectacle. His delicate consideration prompted him to spare his venerable mother all knowledge of his illness. He wrote to her every month in his customary cheerful way; and, in sending her the latest volumes of his poetry, he caused a separate copy always to be printed, from which all allusions to his malady were expunged. "For that matter," he said, "that any son could be as wretched and miserable as I, no mother would believe."

Alas! if he had known how much more eloquent and noble a refutation his life would afford than his mistaken passionate response to the imputations of his enemies! Is this patient martyr the man of whom Börne wrote: "with his sybarite nature, the fall of a rose-leaf can disturb Heine's slumber. He whom all asperities fatigue, whom all discords trouble, let such a one neither move nor think let him go to bed and shut his eyes."

Only in his last poems, which were not to be published till after his death, has Heine given free vent to the bitterness of his anguish. During the long sleepless night when he lay writhing with pain or exhausted by previous paroxysms, his mind, preternaturally clear and vigorous, conceived the glowing fantasies of the Romancero, or the Job-like lamentations of the Lazarus poems. This mental exercise was his protection against insanity: and the thought of his cherished wife, he affirmed, was his only safeguard against the delirious desire to seize the morphine bottle by his side, and with one draught put an end to his agony. On the night of the 16th of February, 1856, came the long-craved release and on the 20th of February without mass or "Kaddish," according to his express wish, he was buried in the cemetery of Montmartre.

HEINRICH HEINE

EARLY POEMS

SONNETS TO MY MOTHER,

I.

I have been wont to bear my forehead high
My stubborn temper yields with no good grace.
The king himself might look me in the face,
And yet I would not downward cast mine eye.
But I confess, dear mother, openly,
However proud my haughty spirit swell,
When I within thy blessed presence dwell,
Oft am I smit with shy humility.
Is it thy soul, with secret influence,
Thy lofty soul piercing all shows of sense,
Which soareth, heaven-born, to heaven again?
Or springs it from sad memories that tell
How many a time I caused thy dear heart pain,
Thy gentle heart, that loveth me so well!

II.

In fond delusion once I left thy side;
Unto the wide world's end I fain would fare,
To see if I might find Love anywhere,
And lovingly embrace Love as a bride.
Love sought I in all paths, at every gate;
Oft and again outstretching suppliant palms,
I begged in vain of Love the slightest alms,

But the world laughed and offered me cold hate.
Forever I aspired towards Love, forever
Towards Love, and ne'ertheless I found Love never,
And sick at heart, homeward my steps did move.
And lo! thou comest forth to welcome me;
And that which in thy swimming eyes I see,
That is the precious, the long-looked-for Love.

THE SPHINX.

This is the old enchanted wood,
Sweet lime trees scent the wind;
The glamor of the moon has cast
A spell upon my mind.
Onward I walk, and as I walk
Hark to that high, soft strain!
That is the nightingale, she sings,
Of love and of love's pain.
She sings of love and of love's pain,
Of laughter and of tears.
So plaintive her carol, so joyous her sobs,
I dream of forgotten years.
Onward I walk, and as I walk,
There stands before mine eyes
A castle proud on an open lawn,
Whose gables high uprise.
With casements closed, and everywhere
Sad silence in court and halls,
It seemed as though mute death abode
Within those barren walls.
Before the doorway crouched a sphinx,
Half horror and half grace;
With a lion's body, a lion's claws,
And a woman's breast and face.
A woman fair! The marble glance
Spake wild desire and guile.
The silent lips were proudly curled
In a confident, glad smile.
The nightingale, she sang so sweet,
I yielded to her tone.
I touched, I kissed the lovely face,
And lo, I was undone!
The marble image stirred with life,

The stone began to move;
She drank my fiery kisses' glow
With panting thirsty love.
She well nigh drank my breath away;
And, lustful still for more,
Embraced me, and my shrinking flesh
With lion claws she tore.
Oh, rapturous martyrdom! ravishing pain!
Oh, infinite anguish and bliss!
With her horrible talons she wounded me,
While she thrilled my soul with a kiss.
The nightingale sang: "Oh beautiful sphinx.
Oh love! what meaneth this?
That thou minglest still the pangs of death
With thy most peculiar bliss?
Thou beautiful Sphinx, oh solve for me
This riddle of joy and tears!
I have pondered it over again and again,
How many thousand years!"

DONNA CLARA.

In the evening through her garden
Wanders the Alcalde's daughter;
Festal sounds of drum and trumpet
Ring out hither from the castle.
"I am weary of the dances,
Honeyed words of adulation
From the knights who still compare me
To the sun, with dainty phrases.
"Yes, of all things I am weary,
Since I first beheld by moonlight,
Him my cavalier, whose zither
Nightly draws me to my casement.
"As he stands, so slim and daring,
With his flaming eyes that sparkle
From his nobly-pallid features,
Truly he St. George resembles."
Thus went Donna Clara dreaming,
On the ground her eyes were fastened,
When she raised them, lo! before her
Stood the handsome, knightly stranger.
Pressing hands and whispering passion,

These twain wander in the moonlight.
Gently doth the breeze caress them,
The enchanted roses greet them.
The enchanted roses greet them,
And they glow like love's own heralds;
"Tell me, tell me, my belovèd,
Wherefore, all at once thou blushest."
"Gnats were stinging me, my darling,
And I hate these gnats in summer,
E'en as though they were a rabble
Of vile Jews with long, hooked noses."
"Heed not gnats nor Jews, belovèd,"
Spake the knight with fond endearments.
From the almond-tree dropped downward
Myriad snowy flakes of blossoms.
Myriad snowy flakes of blossoms
Shed around them fragrant odors.
"Tell me, tell me, my belovèd,
Looks thy heart on me with favor?"
"Yes, I love thee, oh my darling,
And I swear it by our Savior,
Whom the accursèd Jews did murder
Long ago with wicked malice."
"Heed thou neither Jews nor Savior,"
Spake the knight with fond endearments;
Far-off waved as in a vision
Gleaming lilies bathed in moonlight.
Gleaming lilies bathed in moonlight
Seemed to watch the stars above them.
"Tell me, tell me, my belovèd,
Didst thou not erewhile swear falsely?"
"Naught is false in me, my darling,
E'en as in my bosom floweth
Not a drop of blood that's Moorish,
Neither of foul Jewish current."
"Heed not Moors nor Jews, belovèd,"
Spake the knight with fond endearments.
Then towards a grove of myrtles
Leads he the Alcalde's daughter.
And with love's slight, subtle meshes,
He hath trapped her and entangled;
Brief their words, but long their kisses,
For their hearts are overflowing.

What a melting bridal carol,
Sings the nightingale, the pure one!
How the fire-flies in the grasses
Trip their sparkling, torch-light dances!
In the grove the silence deepens;
Naught is heard save furtive rustling
Of the swaying myrtle branches,
And the breathing of the flowers.
But the sound of drum and trumpet
Burst forth sudden from the castle.
Rudely they awaken Clara,
Pillowed on her lover's bosom.
"Hark, they summon me, my darling.
But before I go, oh tell me,
Tell me what thy precious name is,
Which so closely thou hast hidden."
And the knight, with gentle laughter,
Kissed the fingers of his donna,
Kissed her lips and kissed her forehead,
And at last these words he uttered:
"I, Señora, your belovèd,
Am the son of the respected
Worthy, erudite Grand Rabbi,
Israel of Saragossa!"

DON RAMIRO.

"Donna Clara! Donna Clara!
Hotly-loved through years of passion!
Thou hast wrought me mine undoing,
And hast wrought it without mercy!
"Donna Clara! Donna Clara!
Still the gift of life is pleasant.
But beneath the earth 'tis frightful,
In the grave so cold and darksome.
"Donna Clara! Laugh, be merry,
For to-morrow shall Fernando
Greet thee at the nuptial altar.
Wilt thou bid me to the wedding?"
"Don Ramiro! Don Ramiro!
Very bitter sounds thy language,
Bitterer than the stars' decrees are,
Which bemock my heart's desire.

"Don Ramiro! Don Ramiro!
Cast aside thy gloomy temper.
In the world are many maidens,
But us twain the Lord hath parted.
"Don Ramiro, thou who bravely
Many and many a man hast conquered,
Conquer now thyself, to-morrow
Come and greet me at my wedding."
"Donna Clara! Donna Clara!
Yes, I swear it. I am coming.
I will dance with thee the measure.
Now good-night! I come to-morrow."
"So good-night!" The casement rattled,
Sighing neath it, stood Ramiro.
Long he stood a stony statue,
Then amidst the darkness vanished.
After long and weary struggling,
Night must yield unto the daylight.
Like a many-colored garden,
Lies the city of Toledo.
Palaces and stately fabrics
Shimmer in the morning sunshine.
And the lofty domes of churches
Glitter as with gold incrusted.
Humming like a swarm of insects,
Ring the bells their festal carol.
With sweet tones the sacred anthem
From each house of God ascendeth.
But behold, behold! beyond there,
Yonder from the market-chapel,
With a billowing and a swaying,
Streams the motley throng of people.
Gallant knights and noble ladies,
In their holiday apparel;
While the pealing bells ring clearly,
And the deep-voiced organ murmurs.
But a reverential passage
In the people's midst is opened,
For the richly-clad young couple,
Donna Clara, Don Fernando.
To the bridegroom's palace-threshold,
Wind the waving throngs of people;
There the wedding feast beginneth,

Pompous in the olden fashion.
Knightly games and open table,
Interspersed with joyous laughter,
Quickly flying, speed the hours,
Till the night again hath fallen.
And the wedding-guests assemble
For the dance within the palace,
And their many-colored raiment
Glitters in the light of tapers.
Seated on a lofty dais,
Side by side, are bride and bridegroom,
Donna Clara, Don Fernando,
And they murmur sweet love-whispers.
And within the hall wave brightly
All the gay-decked streams of dancers;
And the rolling drums are beaten.
Shrill the clamorous trumpet soundeth.
"Wherefore, wherefore, beauteous lady,
Are thy lovely glances fastened
Yonder in the hall's far corner?"
In amazement asked Fernando.
"See'st thou not, oh Don Fernando,
Yonder man in sable mantle?"
And the knight spake, kindly smiling,
"Why, 'tis nothing but a shadow."
But the shadow drew anear them,
'Twas a man in sable mantle.
Clara knows at once Ramiro,
And she greets him, blushing crimson.
And the dance begins already,
Gaily whirl around the dancers
In the waltz's reckless circles,
Till the firm floor creaks and trembles.
"Yes, with pleasure, Don Ramiro,
I will dance with thee the measure;
But in such a night-black mantle
Thou shouldst never have come hither."
With fixed, piercing eyes, Ramiro
Gazes on the lovely lady.
Then embracing her, speaks strangely,
"At thy bidding I came hither."
In the wild whirl of the measure,
Press and turn the dancing couple,

And the rolling drums are beaten,
Shrill the clamorous trumpet soundeth.
"White as driven snow thy cheeks are!"
Whispers Clara, inly trembling.
"At thy bidding I came hither,"
Hollow ring Ramiro's accents.
In the hall the tapers flicker,
With the eddying stream of dancers,
And the rolling drums are beaten,
Shrill the clamorous trumpet soundeth.
"Cold as ice I feel thy fingers,"
Whispers Clara, thrilled with terror.
"At thy bidding I came hither."
And they rush on in the vortex.
"Leave me, leave me, Don Ramiro!
Like a corpse's scent thy breath is."
Once again the gloomy sentence,
"At thy bidding I came hither."
And the firm floor glows and rustles,
Merry sound the horns and fiddles;
Like a woof of strange enchantment,
All within the hall is whirling.
"Leave me, leave me, Don Ramiro!"
All is waving and revolving.
Don Ramiro still repeateth,
"At thy bidding I came hither."
"In the name of God, begone then!"
Clara shrieked, with steadfast accent.
And the word was scarcely spoken,
When Ramiro had evanished.
Clara stiffens! deathly pallid,
Numb with cold, with night encompassed.
In a swoon the lovely creature
To the shadowy realm is wafted.
But the misty slumber passes,
And at last she lifts her eyelids.
Then again from sheer amazement
Her fair eyes at once she closes.
For she sees she hath not risen,
Since the dance's first beginning.
Still she sits beside the bridegroom,
And he speaks with anxious question.
"Say, why waxed thy cheek so pallid?

Wherefore filled thine eyes with shadows?"
"And Ramiro?" stammers Clara,
And her tongue is glued with horror.
But with deep and serious furrows
Is the bridegroom's forehead wrinkled.
"Lady, ask not bloody tidings
Don Ramiro died this morning."

TANNHÄUSER.
A LEGEND.

I.

Good Christians all, be not entrapped
In Satan's cunning snare.
I sing the lay of Tannhäuser,
To bid your souls beware.
Brave Tannhäuser, a noble knight,
Would love and pleasure win.
These lured him to the Venusberg.
Seven years he bode therein.
"Dame Venus, loveliest of dames,
Farewell, my life, my bride.
Oh give me leave to part from thee,
No longer may I bide."
"My noble knight, my Tannhäuser,
Thou'st kissed me not to-day.
Come, kiss me quick, and tell me now,
What lack'st thou here, I pray?
"Have I not poured the sweetest wine
Daily for thee, my spouse?
And have I not with roses, dear,
Each day enwreathed thy brows?"
"Dame Venus, loveliest of dames,
My soul is sick, I swear,
Of kisses, roses and sweet wine,
And craveth bitter fare.
"We have laughed and jested far too much,
And I yearn for tears this morn.
Would that my head no rose-wreath wore,
But a crown of sharpest thorn."
"My noble knight, my Tannhäuser,
To vex me thou art fain.

Hast thou not sworn a thousand times
To leave me never again?
"Come! to my chamber let us go;
Our love shall be secret there.
And thy gloomy thoughts shall vanish at sight
Of my lily-white body fair."
"Dame Venus, loveliest of dames,
Immortal thy charms remain.
As many have loved thee ere to-day,
So many shall love again.
"But when I think of the heroes and gods,
Who feasted long ago,
Upon thy lily-white body fair,
Then sad at heart I grow.
Thy lily-white body filleth me
With loathing, for I see
How many more in years to come
Shall enjoy thee, after me."
"My noble knight, my Tannhäuser,
Such words thou should'st not say.
Far liefer had I thou dealt'st me a blow,
As often ere this day.
"Far liefer had I thou should'st strike me low,
Than such an insult speak;
Cold, thankless Christian that thou art,
Thus the pride of my heart to break.
"Because I have loved thee far too well,
To hear such words is my fate,
Farewell! I give thee free leave to go.
Myself, I open the gate!"

II.

In Rome, in Rome, in the holy town,
To the music of chimes and of song,
A stately procession moves, the Pope
Strides in the midst of the throng.
This is the pious Pope Urbain;
The triple crown he wears,
The crimson robe, and many a lord
The train of his garment bears.
"Oh, holy Father, Pope Urbain,
I have a tale to tell;

I stir not hence, till thou shrivest me,
And savest me from hell."
The people stand in a circle near,
And the priestly anthems cease;
Who is the pilgrim wan and wild,
Who falleth upon his knees?
"Oh, holy Father, Pope Urbain,
Who canst bind and loose as well,
Now save me from the evil one,
And from the pains of hell.
"I am the noble Tannhäuser,
Who love and lust would win,
These lured me to the Venusberg,
Seven years I bode therein.
"Dame Venus is a beauteous dame,
Her charms have a subtle glow.
Like sunshine with fragrance of flowers blent
Is her voice so soft and low.
"As the butterfly flutters anigh a flower,
From its delicate chalice sips,
In such wise ever fluttered my soul
Anigh to her rosy lips.
"Her rich black ringlets floating loose,
Her noble face enwreath.
When once her large eyes rest on thee,
Thou canst not stir nor breathe.
"When once her large eyes rest on thee,
With chains thou art bounden fast;
'Twas only in sorest need I chanced
To flee from her hill at last.
"From her hill at last I have escaped,
But through all the livelong day,
Those beautiful eyes still follow me.
'Come back!' they seem to say.
"A lifeless ghost all day I pine,
But at night I dream of my bride,
And then my spirit awakes in me.
She laughs and sits by my side.
"How hearty, how happy, how reckless her laugh!
How the pearly white teeth outpeep!
Ah! when I remember that laugh of hers,
Then sudden tears must I weep.
"I love her, I love her with all my might,

And nothing my love can stay,
'Tis like to a rushing cataract,
Whose force no man can sway.
"For it dashes on from cliff to cliff,
And roareth and foameth still.
Though it break its neck a thousand times,
Its course it would yet fulfill.
"Were all of the boundless heavens mine,
I would give them all to her,
I would give her the sun, I would give her the moon
And each star in its shining sphere.
"I love her, I love her with all my might,
With a flame that devoureth me.
Can these be already the fires of hell,
That shall glow eternally?
"Oh, holy Father, Pope Urbain,
Who canst bind and loose as well,
Now save me from the evil one,
And from the pains of hell!"
Sadly the Pope upraised his hand,
And sadly began to speak:
"Tannhäuser, most wretched of all men,
This spell thou canst not break.
"The devil called Venus is the worst
Amongst all we name as such.
And nevermore canst thou be redeemed
From the beautiful witch's clutch.
"Thou with thy spirit must atone
For the joys thou hast loved so well;
Accursed art thou! thou are condemned
Unto everlasting hell!"

III.

So quickly fared Sir Tannhäuser,
His feet were bleeding and torn
Back to the Venusberg he came,
Ere the earliest streak of morn.
Dame Venus, awakened from her sleep,
From her bed upsprang in haste.
Already she hath with her arms so white
Her darling spouse embraced.
Forth from her nose outstreams the blood,

The tears from her eyelids start;
She moistens the face of her darling spouse
With the tears and blood of her heart.
The knight lay down upon her bed,
And not a word he spake;
Dame Venus to the kitchen went
A bowl of broth to make.
She gave him broth, she gave him bread,
She bathed his wounded feet;
She combed for him his matted hair,
And laughed so low and sweet:
"My noble knight, my Tannhäuser,
Long hast thou left my side.
Now tell me in what foreign lands
So long thou couldst abide."
"Dame Venus, loveliest of dames,
I tarried far from home.
In Rome I had some business, dear,
But quickly back have come.
"On seven hills great Rome is built,
The Tiber flows to the sea.
And while in Rome I saw the Pope;
He sent his love to thee.
"Through Florence led my journey home,
Through Milan, too, I passed;
And glad at heart, through Switzerland
I clambered back at last.
"But as I went across the Alps,
The snow began to fall;
Below, the blue lakes smiled on me;
I heard the eagles call.
"When I upon St. Gothard stood,
I heard the Germans snore;
For softly slumbered there below
Some thirty kings and more.
"To Frankfort I on Schobbas came,
Where dumplings were my food.
They have the best religion there:
Goose-giblets, too, are good.
"In Weimar, the widowed muse's seat,
Midst general grief I arrive.
The people are crying 'Goethe's dead,
And Eckermann's still alive!'"[A]

[A] There are eight more verses to this poem, which I take the liberty of omitting.
E. L.

IN THE UNDERWORLD.

I.

"O to be a bachelor!"
Pluto now forever sighs.
"In my marriage miseries,
I perceive, without a wife
Hell was not a hell before.
"O to be a bachelor!
Since my Proserpine is mine,
Daily for my grave I pine,
When she raileth I can hear
Barking Cerberus no more.
"My poor heart needs rest and ease,
In the realm of shades I cry,
No lost soul is sad as I.
Sisyphus I envy now,
And the fair Danaïdes."

II.

In the realm of shades, on a throne of gold,
By the side of her royal spouse, behold
Fair Proserpine,
With gloomy mien,
While deep sighs upheave her bosom.
"The roses, the passionate song I miss
Of the nightingale; yea, and the sun's warm kiss.
Midst the Lemur's dread,
And the ghostly dead,
Now withers my life's young blossom.
"I am fast in the yoke of marriage bound
To this cursèd rat-hole underground.
Through my window at night,
Peers each ghostly sprite,
And the Styx murmurs lower and lower.
"To-day I have Charon invited to dinner,
He is bald, and his limbs they grow thinner and thinner,

And the judges, beside,
Of the dead, dismal-eyed,
In such company I shall grow sour."

III.

Whilst their grievance each is venting
In the underworld below,
Ceres, on the earth lamenting,
Wrathful wanders to and fro.
With no hood in sloven fashion,
Neither mantle o'er her gown,
She declaims that lamentation
Unto all of us well-known;
"Is the blessed spring-tide here?
Has the earth again grown young?
Green the sunny hills appear,
And the icy band is sprung.
"Mirrored from the clear blue river.
Zeus, unclouded, laugheth out,
Softer zephyr's wings now quiver,
Buds upon the fresh twig sprout."
In the hedge a new refrain;
Call the Oreads from the shore,
"All thy flowers come again,
But thy daughter comes no more."
Ah, how many weary days
I have sought o'er wide earth's space.
Titan, all thy sunny rays
I have sent on her dear trace.
Yet not one renews assurance
Of the darling face I wot,
Day, that finds all things, the durance
Of my lost one, findeth not.
"Hast thou ravished, Zeus, my daughter?
Or, love-smitten by her charms,
Hath, o'er Orcus's night-black water,
Pluto snatched her in his arms?
"Who towards that gloomy strand
Herald of my grief will be?
Ever floats the bark from land,
Bearing phantoms ceaselessly.
"Closed those shadowy fields are ever

Unto any blessèd sight.
Since the Styx hath been a river,
It hath borne no living wight.
"There are thousand stairs descending,
But not one leads upward there.
To her tears no token lending,
At the anxious mother's prayer."

IV.

I will grant thee, what so dear is,
I myself so much have borne.
Take thou comfort. We will fairly
Thy child's ownership divide;
And for six moons shall she yearly
In the upper world abide.
Help thee through long summer hours
In thy husbandry affairs;
Binding up for thee the flowers,
While a new straw-hat she wears.
She will dream when twilight pleasant
Colors all the sky with rose;
When by brooks some clownish peasant
Sweetly on his sheep's pipe blows.
Not a harvest dance without her,
She will frisk with Jack and Bess;
Midst the geese and calves about her
She will prove a lioness.
Hail, sweet rest! I breathe free, single,
Here in Orcus far from strife,
Punch with Lethe I will mingle,
And forget I have a wife.

V.

At times thy glance appeareth to importune,
As though thou didst some secret longing prove.
Alas, too well I know it, thy misfortune
A life frustrated, a frustrated love.
How sad thine eyes are! Yet have I no power
To give thee back thy youth with pleasure rife;
Incurably thy heart must ache each hour
For love frustrated and frustrated life.

THE VALE OF TEARS.

The night wind through the crannies pipes,
And in the garret lie
Two wretched creatures on the straw,
As gaunt as poverty.
And one poor creature speaks and says,
"Embrace me with thine arm,
And press thy mouth against my mouth,
Thy breath will keep me warm."
The other starveling speaks and says,
"When I look into thine eyes
Pain, cold and hunger disappear,
And all my miseries."
They kissed full oft, still more they wept,
Clasped hands, sighed deep and fast;
They often laughed, they even sang,
And both were still at last.
With morning came the coroner,
And brought a worthy leech,
On either corpse to certify
The cause of death of each.
The nipping weather, he affirmed,
Had finished the deceased.
Their empty stomachs also caused,
Or hastened death at last.
He added that when frost sets in
'Tis needful that the blood
Be warmed with flannels; one should have,
Moreover, wholesome food.

SOLOMON.

Dumb are the trumpets, cymbals, drums and shawms to-night,
The angel shapes engirdled with the sword,
About the royal tent keep watch and ward,
Six thousand to the left, six thousand to the right.
They guard the king from evil dreams, from death.
Behold! a frown across his brow they view.
Then all at once, like glimmering flames steel-blue,
Twelve thousand brandished swords leap from the sheath.
But back into their scabbards drop the swords

Of the angelic host; the midnight pain
Hath vanished, the king's brow is smooth again;
And hark! the royal sleeper's murmured words:
"O Shulamite, the lord of all these lands am I,
This empire is the heritage I bring,
For I am Judah's king and Israel's king;
But if thou love me not, I languish and I die."

MORPHINE.

Marked is the likeness 'twixt the beautiful
And youthful brothers, albeit one appear
Far paler than the other, more serene;
Yea, I might almost say, far comelier
Than his dear brother, who so lovingly
Embraced me in his arms. How tender, soft
Seemed then his smile, and how divine his glance!
No wonder that the wreath of poppy-flowers
About his head brought comfort to my brow,
And with its mystic fragrance soothed all pain
From out my soul. But such delicious balm
A little while could last. I can be cured
Completely only when that other youth,
The grave, pale brother, drops at last his torch.
Lo, sleep is good, better is death in sooth
The best of all were never to be born.

SONG.

Oft in galleries of art
Thou hast seen a knight perchance,
Eager for the wars to start,
Well-equipped with shield and lance.
Him the frolic loves have found,
Robbed him of his sword and spear,
And with chains of flowers have bound
Their unwilling chevalier.
Held by such sweet hindrances,
Wreathed with bliss and pain, I stay,
While my comrades in the press
Wage the battle of the day.

SONG.

Night lay upon my eyelids,
About my lips earth clave;
With stony heart and forehead
I lay within my grave.
How long I cannot reckon,
I slept in that strait bed;
I woke and heard distinctly
A knocking overhead.
"Wilt thou not rise, my Henry?
The eternal dawn is here;
The dead have re-arisen,
Immortal bliss is near."
"I cannot rise, my darling,
I am blinded to the day.
Mine eyes with tears, thou knowest,
Have wept themselves away."
"Oh, I will kiss them, Henry,
Kiss from thine eyes the night.
Thou shalt behold the angels
And the celestial light."
"I cannot rise, my darling,
My blood is still outpoured
Where thou didst wound my heart once
With sharp and cruel word."
"I'll lay my hand, dear Henry,
Upon thy heart again.
Then shall it cease from bleeding.
And stilled shall be its pain."
"I cannot rise, my darling,
My head is bleeding see!
I shot myself, thou knowest,
When thou wast reft from me."
"Oh, with my hair, dear Henry,
I'll staunch the cruel wound,
And press the blood-stream backward;
Thou shalt be whole and sound."
So kind, so sweet she wooed me,
I could not say her nay;
I tried to rise and follow,
And clasp my loving may.
Then all my wounds burst open,
From head and breast outbreak

The gushing blood in torrents
And lo, I am awake!

SONG.

Death comes, and now must I make known
That which my pride eternally
Prayed to withhold; for thee, for thee,
My heart has throbbed for thee alone.
The coffin waits! within my grave
They drop me soon, where I shall rest.
But thou, Marie, shalt beat thy breast,
And think of me, and weep and rave.
And thou shalt wring thy hands, my friend.
Be comforted! it is our fate,
Our human fate, the good and great
And fair must have an evil end.

HOMEWARD BOUND 1823 TO 1824

TO FREDERIKA VARNHAGEN VON ENSE, THE SONGS OF HOMEWARD BOUND ARE DEDICATED IN JOYFUL HOMAGE BY THE AUTHOR HEINRICH HEINE.

HOMEWARD BOUND.

I.

In my life, too full of shadows,
Beamed a lovely vision bright.
Now the lovely vision's vanished,
I am girt about by night.
Little children in the darkness
Feel uneasy fears erelong,
And, to chase away their terrors,
They will sing aloud a song.
I, a foolish child, am singing
Likewise in the dark apart.
If my homely lay lack sweetness,
Yet it cheers my anxious heart.

II.

I know not what spell is o'er me,
That I am so sad to day;
An old myth floats before me
I cannot chase it away.

The cool air darkens, and listen,
How softly flows the Rhine!
The mountain peaks still glisten
Where the evening sunbeams shine.
The fairest maid sits dreaming
In radiant beauty there.
Her gold and her jewels are gleaming.
She combeth her golden hair.
With a golden comb she is combing;
A wondrous song sings she.
The music quaint in the gleaming,
Hath a powerful melody.
It thrills with a passionate yearning
The boatman below in the night.
He heeds not the rocky reef's warning,
He gazes alone on the height.
I think that the waters swallowed
The boat and the boatman anon.
And this, with her singing unhallowed,
The Lorelei hath done.

III.

My heart, my heart is heavy,
Though merrily glows the May.
Out on the ancient bastion,
Under the lindens, I stay.
Below me the calm blue waters
Of the quiet town-moat shine;
A boy in his boat rows past me,
He whistles and drops his line.
And yonder the cheerful colors,
And tiny figures, one sees,
Of people, and villas, and gardens,
And cattle, and meadows, and trees.
Young women are bleaching linen;
They leap in the grass anear.
The mill-wheel rains showers of diamonds,
Its far away buzz I hear.
Above on the gray old tower
Stands the sentry house of the town,
And a scarlet-coated fellow
Goes pacing up and down.

He toys with his shining musket
That gleams in the sunset red,
Presenting and shouldering arms now
I wish he would shoot me dead.

IV.

In tears through the woods I wander.
The thrush is perched on the bough:
She springs and sings up yonder
"Oh, why so sad art thou?"
The swallows, thy sisters, are able
My dear, to answer thee.
They built clever nests in the gable,
Where sweetheart's windows be.

V.

The night is wet and stormy,
And void of stars the sky;
'Neath the rustling trees of the forest
I wander silently.
There flickers a lonely candle
In the huntsman's lodge to-night.
It shall not tempt me thither;
It burns with a sullen light.
There sits the blind old granny,
In the leathern arm-chair tall,
Like a statue, stiff, uncanny
And speaketh not at all.
And to and fro strides, cursing,
The ranger's red haired son,
With angry, scornful laughter
Flings to the wall his gun.
The beautiful spinner weepeth,
And moistens with tears her thread.
At her feet her father's pointer,
Whimpering, crouches his head.

VI.

When I met by chance in my travels
All my sweetheart's family,

Papa, mamma, little sister
Most cordially greeted me.
About my health they inquired;
Nor even did they fail
To say I was nowise altered,
Only a trifle pale.
I asked after aunts and cousins,
And many a dull old bore.
And after the dear little poodle,
That barked so softly of yore.
And how was my married sweetheart?
I asked them soon. They smiled,
And in friendliest tone made answer
She was soon to have a child.
And I lisped congratulations,
And begged, when they should see,
To give her the kindest greetings,
A thousand times for me.
Burst forth the baby-sister,
"That dear little dog of mine
Went mad when he grew bigger,
And we drowned him in the Rhine."
The child resembles my sweetheart,
The same old laugh has she;
Her eyes are the same ones over,
That wrought such grief for me.

VII.

We sat in the fisher's cabin,
Looking out upon the sea.
Then came the mists of evening,
Ascending silently.
The lights began in the lighthouse
One after one to burn,
And on the far horizon
A ship we could still discern.
We spake of storm and shipwreck,
The sailor and how he thrives,
And how betwixt heaven and ocean,
And joy and sorrow he strives.
We spake of distant countries,
South, North, and everywhere,

And of the curious people,
And curious customs there;
The fragrance and light of the Ganges,
That giant-trees embower,
Where a beautiful tranquil people
Kneel to the lotus flower;
Of the unclean folk in Lapland,
Broad-mouthed and flat-headed and small,
Who cower upon the hearthstone,
Bake fish, and cackle and squall.
The maidens listened gravely,
Then never a word was said,
The ship we could see no longer;
It was far too dark o'erhead.

VIII.

Thou fairest fisher maiden,
Row thy boat to the land.
Come here and sit beside me,
Whispering, hand in hand.
Lay thy head on my bosom,
And have no fear of me;
For carelessly thou trustest
Daily the savage sea.
My heart is like the ocean,
With storm and ebb and flow,
And many a pearl lies hidden
Within its depths below.

IX.

The moon is up, and brightly
Beams o'er the waters vast.
I clasp my darling tightly;
Our hearts are beating fast.
In the dear child's bosom, nestling,
Alone I lie on the sand.
"Hear'st thou the wild winds rustling?
Why trembles thy foam-white hand?"
"That is no wild wind sighing,
That is the mermaid's lay;
And they are my sisters crying,

Whom the sea swallowed one day."

X.

Up amidst the clouds, the moon,
Like a giant orange, beams,
O'er the gray sea shining down,
With broad stripes and golden gleams.
And I pace the shore alone,
Where the billows white are broken.
Many a tender word I hear,
Words within the water spoken.
Ah, the night is far too long,
And my heart throbs fast for pleasure.
Beautiful undines, come forth!
Sing and dance your magic measure.
Take my body and my soul:
On your lap my head shall rest.
Sing to death, caress to death;
Kiss the life from out my breast.

XI.

All in gray clouds closely muffled,
Now the high gods sleep together,
And I listen to their snoring.
Here below 'tis stormy weather.
Stormy weather, raging tempest
Soon the helpless vessel shatters.
Who these furious winds can bridle?
Who can curb the lordless waters?
I can ne'er control the tempest,
Over deck and masthead sweeping;
I will wrap me in my mantle,
And will sleep as gods are sleeping.

XII.

The night wind draws his trousers on,
His foam-white hose once more;
He wildly whips the waves anon,
They howl, and rage, and roar.
From yon dark height, with frantic might,

The rain pours ceaselessly.
It seems as if the ancient night
Would drown the ancient sea.
Anigh the mast the sea-mew screams,
With hoarse shrieks, flying low.
Its every cry an omen seems,
A prophecy of woe.

XIII.

The storm for a dance is piping,
With bellow and roar and hiss.
Hurrah! how the ship is tossing,
What a merry wild night is this!
A living mountain of water
The sea upheaves with might.
Here an abyss is yawning;
There towers a foaming height.
And sounds of retching and curses
Forth from the cabin come;
And I, to the mast close clinging,
Long to be safe at home.

XIV.

The evening shades are falling,
The sea-fog spreads with night.
Mysterious waters are calling,
There rises something white.
The mermaid comes from the ocean,
Beside me sitting down;
Her white breast's breathing motion,
I see through the gossamer gown.
And she doth clasp and hold me,
In passionate, painful way.
Too close thou dost enfold me,
Thou lovely water fay!
"Within mine arms I hide thee,
With all my strength enfold,
I warm myself beside thee,
The night is far too cold."
Paler the moon is growing
Through shadowy vapors gray.

Thine eyes with tears are flowing,
Thou lovely water fay!
"With tears they are not flowing.
As I from waves did rise,
Forth from the ocean going,
A drop fell in mine eyes."
The sea-mews moan, entreating,
What does the mad surf say?
Thy heart is wildly beating,
Thou lovely water fay.
"My heart is beating sadly
And wild as ever it can,
Because I love thee madly,
Thou lovely son of man."

XV.

When I before thy dwelling,
In early morning pace,
How gladly in the window
I see thy gentle face.
Thy brown-black eyes in pity,
Mine own eyes, wistful scan,
"Who art thou, and what lack'st thou,
Thou strange, unhappy man?"
I am a German poet,
Of goodly German fame,
When their best names are spoken,
Mine own they are sure to name.
And what I lack, sweet maiden,
Most Germans lack the same.
When men name sharpest sorrows,
Mine own they are sure to name.

XVI.

The sea outspreading glorious,
In the dying sunbeams shone.
We sat by the lonely fisher's house,
We sat there mute and alone.
The waters swell, the mists arise,
The sea-mew flutters past,
And then from out thy loving eyes

The tears come flowing fast.
I see them falling on thy hand.
Upon my knees I sink,
And from the hollow of thy hand
The burning tears I drink.
Since then strange flames my flesh devour,
My spent soul disappears,
The wretched woman in that hour
Poisoned me with her tears.

XVII.

Up yonder on the mountain,
There stands a castle tall;
There dwelt three beauteous maidens,
And I was loved by all.
On Saturday Hetty kissed me,
And Sunday was Julia's day;
On Monday Kunigunda
Nigh hugged my breath away.
On Tuesday, in the castle,
My maidens gave a ball.
The neighboring lords and ladies
Came riding one and all.
But I was not invited.
Amazed they all appeared;
The gossiping aunts and cousins
Remarked the fact, and sneered.

XVIII.

Upon the far horizon
Like a picture of the mist,
Appears the towered city
By the twilight shadows kissed.
The moist, soft breezes ripple
Our boat's wake gray and dark,
With mournful measured cadence
The boatman rows my bark.
The sun from clouds outshining,
Lights up once more the coast.
The very spot it shows me
Where she I loved was lost.

XIX.

All hail to thee, thou fairest
And most mysterious town!
That once inclosed my dearest
Within thy gateways brown.
Speak out, ye towers and portals!
My sweetheart, where is she?
I left her in your keeping;
Ye should my warders be.
The towers are not guilty,
For rooted fast were they.
When sweetheart, with trunks and luggage,
So quickly stole away.
The gates gave willing passage,
With noiseless bars and locks.
A door will always open,
When the adorer knocks.

XX.

I tread the dear familiar path,
The old road I have taken;
I stand before my darling's house,
Now empty and forsaken.
Oh far too narrow is the street,
The roofs seem tottering downward.
The very pavement burns my feet;
I hurry faster onward.

XXI.

Here to her vows I listened,
I tread the empty halls,
And where her tear-drops glistened,
The poisoned serpent crawls.

XXII.

The quiet night broods over roof-tree and steeple;
Within this house dwelt my treasure rare.
'Tis long since I left the town and its people,

But the house stands still on the self-same square.
Here stands, too, a man; toward heaven he gazes,
And he wrings his hands with a wild despair.
I shudder with awe when his face he raises,
For the moonlight shows me mine own self there.
Oh, pale sad creature! my ghost, my double,
Why dost thou ape my passion and tears,
That haunted me here with such cruel trouble,
So many a night in the olden years?

XXIII.

How can'st thou slumber calmly,
Whilst I alive remain?
My olden wrath returneth,
And then I snap my chain.
Know'st thou the ancient ballad
Of that dead lover brave,
Who rose and dragged his lady
At midnight to his grave?
Believe me, I am living;
And I am stronger far,
Most pure, most radiant maiden,
Than all the dead men are.

XXIV.

The maiden sleeps in her chamber,
Where the trembling moonbeams glance,
Without there singeth and ringeth
The melody of a dance.
"I will look just once from the window,
To see who breaks my rest."
A skeleton fiddles before her,
And sings like one possessed.
"To dance with me you promised,
And you have broken your vow.
To-night is a ball in the churchyard,
Come out and dance with me now."
The music bewitches the maiden;
Forth from her home doth she go;
She follows the bony fiddler,
Who sings as he scrapes his bow.

He fiddles, and hops and dances,
And rattles his bones as he plays;
His skull nods grimly and strangely,
In the clear moonlight's rays.

XXV.

I gazed upon her portrait,
While dark dreams filled my brain,
And those beloved features
Began to breathe again.
I saw upon her lips then
A wondrous smile arise,
And as with tears of pity
Glistened once more her eyes.
Adown my cheeks in silence,
The tears came flowing free.
And oh! I cannot believe it,
That thou art lost to me!

XXVI.

I, a most wretched Atlas, the huge world,
The whole huge world of sorrow I must carry.
Yea, the unbearable must bear, though meanwhile
My heart break in my bosom.
Thou haughty heart, thyself hast willed it thus,
Thou would'st be happy, infinitely happy,
Or infinitely wretched, haughty heart!
And lo! now art thou wretched.

XXVII.

The years are coming and going,
Whole races are home to their rest;
But never ceases the passion
That burns within my breast.
Only once more I would see thee,
And make thee a low salaam,
And with my dying breath, murmur:
"I love you still, Madame!"

XXVIII.

I dreamed that the moon looked sadly down,
And the stars with a troubled ray;
I went to my sweetheart's home the town
Lies many a league away.
My longing led me before her door;
I kissed the stone steps brown,
That her feet had touched in the days of yore,
And the trailing hem of her gown.
The night was long, the night was cold,
Ice-cold did the stone steps seem.
In the window her own wan face, behold!
Illumed by the moon's pale beam.

XXIX.

What means this lonely tear-drop
That blurs my troubled sight,
From olden times returning
Back to mine eyes to-night?
Its many glimmering sisters
Are vanished long ago,
In the night and the wind they vanished
With all my joy and my woe.
And like the mists of evening
Did those blue stars depart,
That smiled all joys and sorrows
Into my trusting heart.
Alas! my love, too, melted
Like idle breath one day;
Oh lingering, lonely tear-drop,
Thou also fade away!

XXX.

The pale half-moon of autumn
Through clouds peers doubtfully.
Within the lonely churchyard
The parsonage I see.
The mother reads in her Bible,
The son at the light doth gaze;
One drowsy daughter is nodding,
While another speaks and says:

"Ah me! how dreary the days are!
How dull, and dark, and mean!
Only when there's a funeral
Is anything to be seen."
The mother looks from her Bible:
"Nay, only four in all
Have died since thy father was buried
Without by the churchyard wall."
Then yawns the eldest daughter,
"I will starve no longer here;
I will go to the Count to-morrow,
He is rich, and he loves me dear."
The son bursts out a-laughing:
"At the 'Star' three huntsmen drink deep;
They are making gold, and they promise
To give me their secret to keep."
Toward his lean face, flings the mother
Her Bible, in wrath and grief.
"Out! God-forsaken beggar,
Thou wilt be a common thief!"
They hear a tap on the window,
And behold a beckoning hand.
There in his sable vestments
They see the dead father stand.

XXXI.

To-night is wretched weather,
It snows, and storms, and rains;
Out in the pitch-black darkness
I gaze through the window-panes.
There flickers a lonely candle,
Slow winding down the street;
And a beldame, with her lantern,
Goes hobbling on in the sleet.
I think 'tis for eggs and butter
That she braves this weather wild,
To bake a cake for her daughter,
Her grown-up ailing child.
Who lies at home in her arm-chair,
And sleepily blinks at the light.
Over her beautiful forehead
Her golden curls wave bright.

XXXII.

They think my heart is breaking,
In sorrow's bitter yoke,
I too begin to think it,
As well as other folk.
Thou large-eyed little darling,
Do I not always say
I love thee past all telling
Love gnaws my heart away?
But only in my chamber
I dare express my pain;
For always in thy presence
Quite silent I remain.
For there were evil angels
Who sealed my lips so close.
And oh! from evil angels
Sprang all my wretched woes.

XXXIII.

Ah, those pure white lily fingers,
Once again could I but kiss them,
Press them close against my heart,
Melt away in silent weeping!
Oh, those clearest eyes of violet
Hover day and night before me,
And I ponder o'er the meaning
Of those lovely blue enigmas.

XXXIV.

"Did she ne'er express compassion
For thy tender situation?
Could'st thou never in her glances
Read thy love's reciprocation?
"Could'st thou ne'er surprise the spirit
In her bright eyes unawares?
Yet thou surely art no donkey,
Dearest friend, in these affairs!"

XXXV.

They loved one another, but neither
Confessed a word thereof.
They met with coldest glances,
Though pining away with love.
At last they parted; their spirits
Met but in visions rare.
They are long since dead and buried,
Though scarcely themselves aware.

XXXVI.

And when I lamented my cruel lot,
You yawned in my face and you answered not.
But now that I set it in daintiest rhyme,
You flourish my trumpet all the time.

XXXVII.

I called the devil and he came,
His face with wonder I must scan;
He is not ugly, he is not lame,
He is a delightful, charming man.
A man in the prime of life, in fact,
Courteous, engaging and full of tact.
A diplomat, too, of wide research
Who cleverly talks about state and church.
A little pale, but that is en règle,
For now he is studying Sanscrit and Hegel.
His favorite poet is still Fouqué;
With the brawls of the critics he meddles no more,
For all such things he has given o'er,
Unto his grandmother Hecaté.
He praised my forensic works that he saw,
He had dabbled a little himself in law.
He said he was proud my acquaintance to make,
And should prize my friendship, and bowed as he spake.
And asked if we had not met before
At the house of the Spanish Ambassador?
Then I noted his features line by line,
And found him an old acquaintance of mine.

XXXVIII.

Mortal, sneer not at the devil;
Life's a short and narrow way,
And perdition everlasting
Is no error of the day.
Mortal, pay thy debts precisely,
Life's a long and weary way;
And to-morrow thou must borrow,
As thou borrow'dst yesterday.

XXXIX.

Three holy kings from the land of the West
Go asking whoso passes,
"Where is the road to Bethlehem,
Ye gentle lads and lasses?"
But neither young nor old can tell.
The kings fare patient onward,
They follow a golden star o'erhead,
That bright and kind shines downward.
The star stands still o'er Joseph's house,
Thither the pilgrims bringing;
The oxen low, the Infant cries,
The three wise kings are singing.

XL.

My child, we two were children,
As lively as ever you saw,
We crept into the hencoop,
And we hid there beneath the straw.
And there, like cocks, crowed loudly,
While folk went passing by.
"Kickery-koo!" they fancied,
'Twas really the cock's own cry.
The chests that lay in the courtyard,
With paper we overlaid.
Therein we lived together;
An excellent house we made.
The old cat of our neighbor
Would visit us at whiles;
We gave her bows and curtsies,
And compliments and smiles.

After her health we inquired
Gravely whenever she came.
To many an ancient Tabby
Since then we have done the same.
We talked like grown folks sagely,
And sat there oft and long,
Complaining how all had altered,
Since the days when we were young.
How love and faith and friendship
Had vanished, the world was bare;
How dear were tea and coffee,
And money had grown so rare!
Those childish games are over,
All things roll on with youth,
Money, the world, and the seasons,
And faith and love and truth.

XLI.

My heart is heavy; from the present
It yearns towards those old days again,
When still the world seemed fair and pleasant,
And men lived happy, free from pain.
Now all things seem at six and sevens,
A scramble and a constant dread;
Dead is the Lord God in the heavens,
Below us is the devil dead.
And all folks sad and mournful moving,
Wear such a cross, cold, anxious face;
Were there not still a little loving,
There would not be a resting place.

XLII.

As the moon with splendor pierces
Through the dark cloud-veil of night,
From my darksome Past emerges
Once again a dream of light.
All upon the deck were seated,
Proudly sailing down the Rhine.
Green with June the shores were glowing
In the evening's sunset-shine.
At the feet of a fair lady

Sat I, full of thoughts untold,
O'er her pale and lovely features
Played the sunlight's ruddy gold.
Lutes were ringing, boys were singing,
Wondrous joy on stream and shore.
Blue and bluer grew the heavens,
And the spirit seemed to soar.
Hill and city, wood and meadow,
Glided past in fairy-wise.
And I saw the whole scene mirrored
In the lovely lady's eyes.

XLIII.

In a dream I saw my sweetheart,
A woman harassed with care;
Faded, and haggard, and withered,
The form that had bloomed so fair.
One child in her arms she carried,
And one by the hand she led.
And trouble and poverty plainly
In her eyes and her raiment I read.
Across the square she tottered,
And face to face we stood.
She looked at me, and I spoke then
In quiet but mournful mood.
"Come home with me to my dwelling,
Thou art pale and ill, I think,
And there, with unceasing labor,
I will furnish thee meat and drink.
"And I will serve thee, and cherish
Thy children so wan and mild.
And thyself more dearly than any,
Thou poor, unhappy child.
"Nor will I vex thee by telling
The love that burns in my breast;
And I will weep when thou diest
Over thy place of rest."

XLIV.

"Dearest friend, what may it profit
To repeat the old refrain?

Wilt thou, brooding still above it,
Sitting on love's egg remain!
Ah, it needs incessant watching;
From the shell the chicks have risen.
Clucking, they reward thy hatching,
And this book shall be their prison."

XLV.

Only bear with me in patience,
If the notes of former wrongs
Many a time distinctly echo
In the latest of my songs.
Wait! the slow reverberation
Of my grief will soon depart,
And a spring of new song blossom
In my healed, reviving heart.

XLVI.

'Tis time that, more sober and serious grown,
From folly at last I break free.
I, who so long in comedian's gown,
Have played in the play with thee.
The scenes gaily painted were bright to behold,
And in ultra-romantic tints shone.
My knightly, rich mantle was spangled with gold;
Noblest feelings were ever mine own.
But now with grave trouble my thoughts are beset,
Although from the stage I depart;
And my heart is as wretchedly miserable yet,
As though I still acted my part.
Ah God! all unwitting and wholly in jest,
What I felt and I suffered I told.
I have fought against Death who abode in my breast
Like the dying wrestler of old.

XLVII.

The great king Wiswamitra
In dire distress is now.
He seeks with strife and penance
To win Waschischta's cow.

Oh, great King Wiswamitra,
Oh what an ox art thou!
So much to struggle and suffer,
And only for a cow.

XLVIII.

Heart, my heart, oh, be not shaken!
Bravely bear thy fate. Once more
Shall the coming Spring restore
What the Winter rude hath taken.
How abundant is thy measure!
Still, O world, how fair thou art!
And thou yet may'st love, my heart,
Everything that gives thee pleasure.

XLIX.

Thou seemest like a flower,
So pure and fair and bright;
A melancholy yearning
Steals o'er me at thy sight.
I fain would lay in blessing
My hands upon thy hair,
Imploring God to keep thee,
So bright, and pure, and fair.

L.

Child, I must be very careful,
For thy soul would surely perish,
If the loved heart in thy bosom
Love for me should ever cherish.
But the task proves all too easy,
Strange regrets begin to move me.
Meanwhile many a time I whisper:
"If I could but make her love me!"

LI.

When on my couch reclining,
Buried in pillows and night,
There hovers then before me

A form of grace and light.
As soon as quiet slumber
Has closed my weary eyes,
Then softly does the image
Within my dream arise.
But with my dream at morning,
It never melts away;
For in my heart I bear it
Through all the livelong day.

LII.

Maiden with the lips of scarlet,
Clearest, sweetest eyes that be,
O my darling little maiden,
Ever do I think of thee!
Dreary is the winter evening:
Would that I were in thy home,
Sitting by thee, calmly chatting,
In the cosy little room.
And upon my lips, my darling,
I would press thy small white hand.
I would press and I would moisten
With my tears thy small, white hand.

LIII.

Let the snow without be piled,
Let the howling storm rage wild,
Beating o'er the window-pane,
I will never more complain,
For within my heart bide warm
Spring-tide joy and sweetheart's form.

LIV.

Some to Mary bend the knee,
Others unto Paul and Peter,
I, however, I will worship,
Sun of beauty, only thee.
Kiss me, love me, dearest one,
Be thou gracious, show me favor,
Fairest sun among all maidens,

Fairest maiden under the sun.

LV.

Did not my pallid cheek betray
My love's unhappy fate?
And wilt thou force my haughty lips
To beg and supplicate?
Oh far too haughty are these lips,
They can but kiss and jest.
They speak perchance a scornful word,
While my heart breaks in my breast.

LVI.

Dearest friend, thou art in love,
Tortured with new woes thou art;
Darker grows it in thy brain,
Lighter grows it in thy heart.
Dearest friend, thou art in love,
Though thou hast not yet confessed.
I can see thy flaming heart
Burn already through thy vest.

LVII.

I fain by thee would tarry,
To rest there and to woo;
But thou away must hurry,
Thou hadst too much to do.
I told thee that my spirit
Was wholly bound to thee,
And thou didst laugh to hear it,
And curtsy low to me.
Yea, thou did'st much misuse me,
In all my love's distress,
And even didst refuse me
At last the parting kiss.
I will not for thy glory
Go drown, when all is o'er;
My dear, this same old story
Befell me once before.

LVIII.

Sapphires are those eyes of thine,
So lovely and so sweet,
Thrice blessed is the happy man
Whom they with love will greet.
Thy heart, it is a diamond,
That sheds a splendid light.
Thrice blessed is the happy man
For whom it glows so bright.
As red as rubies are thy lips,
Naught fairer can I prove.
Thrice blessed is the happy man
To whom they whisper love.
Oh, knew I but that happy man,
Could I at last discover,
Deep in the greenwood, all alone
His bliss were quickly over.

LIX.

Lovers' vows, wherefrom thou turnest,
Bound me closely to thy heart,
Now my jest grows sober earnest,
I am pierced by mine own dart.
Laughingly thou stand'st before me
If thou leave me in my need,
All the powers of hell come o'er me,
I shall shoot myself indeed.

LX.

Our life and the world have too fragment-like grown;
To the German Professor I'll hie me anon
Who sets in straight order all things overhurled.
He will draw up a sensible system, I think,
With his nightcap and nightgown he'll stop every chink
In this tumble-down edifice known as the world.

LXI.

Long through my racked and weary brain
Did endless thoughts and dreams revolve;

But now thy lovely eyes, my dear,
Have brought me to a firm resolve.
Within their radiance wise and kind,
Where'er thine eyes shine, I remain.
I could not have believed it true
That I should ever love again.

LXII.

To-night they give a party,
The house is all a-glow.
Above, in the lighted window,
Moves a shadow to and fro.
Thou see'st me not in the darkness,
I stand below, apart.
Still less, my dear, thou seeest
Within my gloomy heart.
My gloomy heart it loves thee;
It breaks for love of thee,
It breaks, and yearns, and bleedeth,
Only thou wilt not see.

LXIII.

I fain would outpour all my sorrows
In a single word to-day.
To the merry winds I would trust it,
They would merrily bear it away.
They would bear it to thee, my darling,
The word of sorrowful grace.
Thou should'st hear it at every hour,
Thou shouldst hear it in every place.
And scarce in the midnight darkness
Shouldst thou close thine eyes in sleep,
Ere my whispered word, it would follow,
Though thy dream were ever so deep.

LXIV.

Thou hast diamonds, and pearls and jewels,
All thy heart covets in store,
And the loveliest eyes under heaven
My darling, what wouldst thou more?

Upon thine eyes, so lovely,
Have I written o'er and o'er
Immortal songs and sonnets
My darling, what wouldst thou more?
And with thine eyes so lovely
Thou hast stung me to the core,
And hast compassed my undoing
My darling, what wouldst thou more?

LXV.

He who for the first time loves,
E'en rejected, is a god.
He who loves a second time,
Unrequited, is a fool.
Such a fool am I, in loving
Once again with no return.
Sun and moon and stars are laughing;
I am laughing too and dying.

LXVI.

They gave me advice, they counseled sense,
They overpowered with compliments.
Patience! they said, and in my need
They'd prove themselves my friends indeed.
Despite their promise to help and protect,
I surely had perished of sheer neglect,
Had there not come a worthy man,
Who bravely to help me now began.
Oh, the worthy man! he gave me to eat;
Such kindness as his I shall never forget.
I long to embrace him, but never can,
For I am myself this excellent man.

LXVII.

This most amiable of fellows
Ne'er enough can honored be.
Ah! to oysters, Rhine-wine, cordial,
Many a time he treated me.
Natty are his hose and trousers,
Nattier his cravat is seen;

And he enters every morning,
Asks me how my health has been.
Of my rich renown he speaketh,
Of my charms and wit displayed.
Zealous, eager seems he ever
To befriend me and to aid.
And at parties in the evening,
With inspired brow and eye,
He declaims before the ladies
My immortal poesy.
How delightfully refreshing
Now-a-days to find still here
Such a youth, when good things surely
More and more do disappear.

LXVIII.

I dreamt I was Almighty God,
And sat within the sky,
And angels sat on either side,
And praised my poetry.
And sweets and pasties there I ate,
And drank the best Tokay,
Worth many a precious florin bright,
Yet had no bill to pay.
No less was I nigh bored to death,
And longed for earth and evil,
And were I not Almighty God,
I fain had been the devil.
"Thou long-legged angel Gabriel,
Make haste; begone from here!
And hither bring my friend Eugene,
The friend I love so dear.
"Within the college seek him not,
But where good wine inspires.
And seek him not in Hedwig Church,
But seek him at Miss Myers'."
Then spreading broad his mighty wings,
The angel doth descend,
And hastens off, and brings me back
Dear Bendel, my good friend.
Lo, youth, I am Almighty God!
The earth is my estate.

Did I not always promise thee
I should be something great?
And I accomplish miracles
That shall thy homage win.
To-day to please thee I shall bless
The city of Berlin.
Behold, the pavements of each street
Now wider, broader, grown!
And to an oyster, fresh and clear,
Transformed is every stone.
A shower of sweet lemonade
Pours down like dew divine.
And through the very gutters flows
The mellowest Rhine wine.
Oh, how the Berlinese rejoice!
They lush o'er such good fare.
The councillors and aldermen
Will drain the gutters bare.
The poets are in ecstasies
At such a feast divine.
The captains and the corporals
Lick up the streaming wine.
The captains and the corporals,
What clever men are they!
They think such miracles as these
Occur not every day.

LXIX.

I left you in the midmost of July,
To-day, my friends in winter I behold.
Then in the heat ye basked so warm and bright,
But now ye have grown cool, yea, even cold.
Soon I depart again, and come once more,
Then shall I find you neither warm nor cold.
And I shall moan lamenting o'er your graves,
And mine own heart shall then be poor and old.

LXX.

Oh, to be chased from lovely lips! and torn
From lovely arms that clasped as in a dream.
I fain had stayed with thee another morn.

Then came the postboy with his tinkling team.
E'en such is life, my child, a constant moan
A constant parting, evermore good-byes,
Could not thy heart cling fast unto mine own?
Couldst thou not hold me steadfast with thine eyes?

LXXI.

All night, in the shadowy post-chaise,
We drove through the winter weather.
We slept on each other's bosoms,
We jested and laughed together.
But how were we both astonished,
When morning bade us stir,
Betwixt us two sat Cupid,
The blindfold passenger.

LXXII.

Lord knows where the reckless creature
Chose her transient stopping-place!
Swearing through the rainy weather,
Everywhere I seek her trace.
I have been to every tavern
Running up and running down,
And of every surly waiter
Made inquiries in the town.
Lo, I see her in yon window!
And she beckons all is well!
Could I guess that you had chosen,
Lady, such a grand hotel?

LXXIII.

Like shadows black the houses
Uprise in long array.
Enveloped in my mantle
I hurry on my way.
The old cathedral-belfry
Chimes midnight grave and slow.
With all her charms and kisses
My love awaits me now.
The moon is my companion,

Kind-beaming from the sky
I reach the house beloved,
And joyously I cry
"I thank thee, trusty servant,
That thou hast cheered my way.
And now, dear moon, I leave thee.
On others shed thy ray.
"And if a lonely lover
Who sings of grief, thou see,
Oh give him such sweet solace
As thou hast given me."

LXXIV.

Wert thou, in sooth, mine honored wife,
Then shouldst thou envied be;
A merry pastime were thy life
All pleasure, mirth, and glee.
And should'st thou scold, and rail and curse,
I'd meekly bear my fate;
But if thou do not praise my verse,
Then shall we separate.

LXXV.

Upon thy snow-white shoulders
I lean my head at rest;
And secretly I hearken
To the yearning of thy breast.
In thy heart hussars blue-coated
Are riding and blowing their horn;
And my darling will surely desert me
With the earliest streak of morn.
And if thou desert me to-morrow,
None the less art thou mine to-day.
And within thine arms so lovely,
Still doubly blest I stay.

LXXVI.

Hussars are blowing their trumpets,
And to thy doors they ride.
A garland of wreathed roses

I bring to thee, my bride.
That were a boisterous household,
Landpests and soldiery!
And in thy little heart, dear,
The goodliest quarters be.

LXXVII.

I, too, in my youth did languish,
Suffered many a bitter anguish,
Burning in love's spell.
Now the price of fuel's higher,
And extinguished is the fire,
Ma foi! and that is well.
Think of this, my youthful beauty,
Dry the stupid tears of duty,
Quell love's stupid, vague alarms.
Since thy life is not yet over,
Oh forget thy former lover,
Ma foi! within mine arms.

LXXVIII.

Dost thou hate me then so fiercely,
Hast thou really changed so blindly?
To the world I shall proclaim it,
Thou could'st treat me so unkindly.
Say, ungrateful lips, how can you
Breathe an evil word of scorning,
Of the very man who kissed you
So sincerely, yestermorning?

LXXIX.

Yes, they are the self-same eyes
That still brighten as I greet her,
Yes, they are the self-same lips
That made all my life seem sweeter.
Yes, it is the very voice,
At whose slightest tones I faltered
But no more the same am I;
I wend homeward strangely altered.
By the fair white arms embraced

With a close and tender passion,
Now I lie upon her heart,
Dull of brain, in cold vexation.

LXXX.

Ye could not understand mine ire
Nor I the tales that ye did tell,
But when we met within the mire,
We knew each other very well.

LXXXI.

But the eunuchs still complained,
When I raised my voice to sing
They complained and they maintained
That it had too harsh a ring.
And they raised with one accord
All their dainty voices clear,
Little crystal trills outpoured
Oh, how pure and fine to hear!
And they sang of love so sweet,
Love's desire and love's full measure,
That the rare artistic treat
Made the ladies weep for pleasure.

LXXXII.

On the walls of Salamanca
Gently sigh the breezes yonder.
Often with my gracious Donna,
There on summer eves I wander.
Round my beauty's slender girdle,
Tenderly mine arm enwreathing,
I can feel with blessed finger
Her proud bosom's haughty breathing.
But I hear an anxious whisper
Through the linden-branches coming,
And below, the somber mill-stream
Murmurs dreams of evil omen.
Ah, Señora, I foresee it!
I shall be expelled forever,
On the walls of Salamanca,

We again shall wander never!

LXXXIII.

Next to me lives Don Henriquez,
He whom folk "the beauty" call;
Neighborly our rooms are parted
Only by a single wall.
Salamanca's ladies flutter
When he strides along the street,
Clinking spurs, mustachoes twirling,
And with hounds about his feet.
But in quiet hours of evening
He will sit at home apart,
His guitar between his fingers,
And sweet dreams within his heart.
Then he smites the chords with passion,
All at once begins to strum.
Ah, like squalling cats his scrapings,
Toll-de-roll and toodle-dum!

LXXXIV.

We scarcely had met ere thy voice and thine eye
Assured me, my darling, that thou wast mine own;
And had not thy mother stood cruelly nigh,
I think I should really have kissed thee anon.
To-morrow again I depart from the town,
And hasten forth on my weary track,
From the window my yellow-haired lass peeps down,
And the friendliest greetings I waft her back.

LXXXV.

Lo, on the mountains the sunbeams' first kiss!
The bells of the herd ring afar on the plain,
My darling, my lambkin, my sun and my bliss,
Oh, fain would I see thee and greet thee again!
I gaze on thy windows with curious eyes.
Farewell, dearest child, I must vanish for thee,
In vain! for the curtain moves not there she lies,
There slumbers she still and dreams about me?

LXXXVI.

In Halle, near the market,
There stand two mighty lions.
Ah, lion-strength of Halle town,
How art thou tamed and broken!
In Halle, near the market,
There stands a mighty giant,
He holds a sword and he never moves,
He is petrified with terror.
In Halle, near the market,
A stately church is standing,
Where the Burschenschaft and the Landsmannschaft
Have plenty of room to worship.

LXXXVII.

Dusky summer-eve declineth
Over wood and verdant meadow,
Golden moon in azure heavens,
Wafting fragrance, softly shineth.
By the brook-side chirps the cricket,
Something stirs within the water,
And the wanderer hears a rustling,
Hears a breathing past the thicket.
In the streamlet, white and slender,
All alone the nymph is bathing,
Beautiful her arms and shoulders
Shimmer in the moonbeams' splendor.

LXXXVIII.

Night enfolds these foreign meadows,
Sick heart, weary limbs caressing.
Ah, thy light athwart the shadows,
Moon, is like a quiet blessing!
Gentle moon, thy mild beams banish
Gloomy terrors where they hover.
All my woes dissolve and vanish,
And mine eyes with dew brim over.

LXXXIX.

Death is like the balmy night,
Life is like the sultry day;
It is dark, and I am sleepy.
I am weary of the light.
O'er my couch a tree doth spring
In its boughs a nightingale
Sings of love, of naught but love,
In my dream I hear him sing.

XC.

"Tell me where's your lovely maiden,
Whom you sang of erst so well,
As a flame that through your bosom
Pierced with rare, enchanted spell."
Ah, that flame is long extinguished!
And my heart is cold above.
And this little book the urn is
For the ashes of my love.

SONGS TO SERAPHINE

I.

In the dreamy wood I wander,
In the wood at even-tide;
And thy slender, graceful figure
Wanders ever by my side.
Is not this thy white veil floating?
Is not that thy gentle face?
Is it but the moonlight breaking
Through the dark fir-branches' space?
Can these tears so softly flowing
Be my very own I hear?
Or indeed, art thou beside me,
Weeping, darling, close anear?

II.

Over all the quiet sea-shore
Shadowing falls the hour of Hesper;
Through the clouds the moon is breaking,
And I hear the billows whisper.
"Can that man who wanders yonder
Be a lover or a dunce?
For he seems so sad and merry,
Sad and merry both at once."
But the laughing moon looks downward,
And she speaks, for she doth know it:

"Yes, he is both fool and lover,
And, to cap it all, a poet!"

III.

Behold! 'tis a foam-white sea-mew
That flutters there on high.
Far over the black night-waters
The moon hangs up in the sky.
The shark and the roach dart forward
For breath as the breeze floats by.
The sea-mew poises and plunges,
The moon hangs up in the sky.
Oh, lovely transient spirit,
How heavy of heart am I!
Too near to thee is the water,
The moon hangs up in the sky.

IV.

In moonlit splendor rests the sea,
The soft waves ripple along.
My heart beats low and heavily,
I think of the ancient song.
The ancient song that quaintly sings
Towns lost in olden times;
And how from the sea's abyss there rings
The sound of prayers and chimes.
But pious prayers and chimes, I ween,
Are offered all in vain.
For that which once hath buried been
May never come back again.

V.

I knew that thou must love me
'Twas long ago made clear.
But thy confession filled me
With deep and secret fear.
I clambered up the mountain,
And sang aloud for glee.
Then while the sun was setting,
I wept beside the sea.

My heart is like the sun, dear,
Yon kindled flame above;
And sinks in large-orbed beauty
Within a sea of love.

VI.

How enviously the sea-mew
Looks after us, my dear;
Because upon thy lips then
So close I pressed mine ear.
He fain would know what issued,
Most curious of birds!
If thou mine ear fulfillest
With kisses or with words.
What through my spirit hisses?
I, too, am sore perplexed!
Thy words, dear, and thy kisses
Are strangely intermixed.

VII.

Shy as a fawn she passed me by;
And, fleet as any heifer,
She clambered on from cliff to cliff,
Her hair flew with the zephyr.
Where to the sea's edge slope the rocks,
I reached her, trembling near it.
Then, softly with the softest words,
I melted her proud spirit.
There we two sat as high as heaven,
And heaven's own rapture drinking.
While in the dark waves far below;
The gradual sun was sinking.
Below us in the deep, dark sea,
The fair sun dropped; then dashing,
The waves broke wildly over him,
With turbulence of passion.
Oh do not weep! he is not dead,
'Neath billows swelling higher;
He has but hidden in my heart,
With all his burning fire.

VIII.

Come, let us build upon this rock,
The Church of God's last lover,
The third New Testament's revealed,
The agony is over.
Refuted is the second book
That fooled us through long ages.
The stupid torture of the flesh
Is not for modern sages.
Hear'st thou the Lord in the dark sea,
With thousand voices speaking?
See'st thou o'erhead the thousand lights
Of God's own glory breaking?
The holy God dwells in the light,
As in the dark abysses.
For God is everything that is:
His breath is in our kisses.

IX.

Gray night broods above the ocean,
Little stars gleam sparkling o'er us.
And the waters' many voices
Chant in deep, protracted chorus.
Hark! the old northwind is playing
On the polished waves of ocean,
That, like tubes of some great organ,
Thrill and stir with sounding motion.
Partly pagan, partly sacred,
Rise these melodies upswelling
Passionately to the heavens,
Where the joyous stars are dwelling.
And the stars wax large and larger,
In bright mazes they are driven,
Large as suns at last revolving,
Through the spaces of vast heaven.
And weird harmonies they warble
With the billows' music blending.
Solar nightingales, they circle
Through the spheres strange concord sending.
And with mighty roar and trembling,
Sky and ocean both are ringing;

And a giant's stormy rapture
Feel I in my bosom springing.

X.

Shadow-love and shadow-kisses,
Life of shadows, wondrous strange!
Shall all hours be sweet as this is,
Silly darling, safe from change?
All things that we clasp and cherish,
Pass like dreams we may not keep.
Human hearts forget and perish,
Human eyes must fall asleep.

XI.

She stood beside the ocean,
And sighed as one oppressed,
With such a deep emotion
The sunset thrilled her breast.
Dear maiden, look more gayly,
This trick is old, thou'lt find.
Before us sinks he daily,
To rise again behind.

XII.

My ship sails forth with sable sails,
Far over the savage sea;
Thou know'st how heavy is my woe,
Yet still thou woundest me.
Thy heart is fickle as the wind,
And flits incessantly.
My ship sails forth with sable sails,
Far over the savage sea.

XIII.

I told nor man, nor woman
How ill you dealt with me;
I came abroad and published it
To the fishes in the sea.
Only upon terra firma

I have left you your good name;
But over all the ocean
Every creature knows your shame.

XIV.

The roaring waves press onward
To reach the strand.
Then swell, and, crashing downward,
Break on the sand.
They roll with surging power,
Nor rest, nor fail
And then ebb slow and slower
Of what avail?

XV.

The Runenstein juts in the sea,
I sit here with my dreams,
The billows wander foamingly;
Winds pipe, the sea-mew screams.
Oh I have loved full many a lass,
And many a worthy fellow,
Where have they gone? The shrill winds pass,
And wandering foams the billow.

XVI.

The waves gleam in the sunshine,
They seem of gold to be.
When I am dead, my brothers,
Oh drop me in the sea.
For dearly have I loved it.
Like cooling balm descends
Upon my heart its current:
We were the best of friends.

TO ANGELIQUE

I.

Now that heaven smiles in favor,
Like a mute shall I still languish,
I, who when unhappy, ever
Sang so much about mine anguish?
Till a thousand striplings haunted
By despair, my notes re-fluted,
And unto the woe I chanted,
Greater evils still imputed.
Oh ye nightingales' sweet choir,
That my bosom holds in capture,
Lift your joyous voices higher,
Let the whole world hear your rapture!

II.

Though thou wert fain to pass me quickly,
Yet backward didst thou look by chance;
Thy wistful lips were frankly parted,
Impetuous scorn was in thy glance.
Would that I ne'er had sought to hold thee,
To touch thy fleeing gown's white train!
The dear mark of thy tiny footprints
Would that I ne'er had found again!
For now thy rare wild charm has vanished,
Like others thou art tame to see,

Intolerably kind and gentle
Alas! thou art in love with me.

III.

Ne'er can I believe, young beauty,
Thy disdainful lips alone:
For such big black eyes as thine are
Virtue never yet did own.
And those brown-streaked lies down-glancing
Say "I love thee!" clearly scanned,
Let thy little white heart kiss me
White heart, dost thou understand?

IV.

From the slightest of emotions,
What a sudden transformation,
To the most unbounded passion,
And the tenderest relation!
Every day it waxes deeper,
My affection for my lady.
I am almost half-persuaded
That I am in love already.
Beautiful her soul: though truly
That's a question of opinion.
I am surer of the beauty
Of the bodily dominion.
Oh that waist! And oh that forehead!
Oh that nose! The sweet enclosure
Of the lovely lips in smiling!
And the bearing's proud composure!

V.

Ah, how fair thou art when frankly
Thou reveal'st thy soul's dimensions,
And thy speech is overflowing
With the noblest of intentions.
When thou tell'st me how thy feelings
Always have been truest, highest,
To the pride within thy bosom
Thou no sacrifice denyest.

Not for millions, thou averrest,
Man could thy pure honor buy,
Ere thou sell thyself for money
Ah, thou wouldst far liefer die.
I before thee stand and listen;
To the end I listen stoutly,
Like a type of faith in silence,
And I fold my hands devoutly.

VI.

I closed my sweetheart's either eye,
And on her mouth I kissed,
Now asking me the reason why
She never gives me rest.
From set of sun till morning rise,
Each hour does she persist,
'Oh wherefore did you close mine eyes,
When on my mouth you kissed?"
I never yet have told her why,
Myself I scarcely wist.
I closed my sweetheart's either eye,
And on her mouth I kissed.

VII.

When I, enraptured by precious kisses,
Rest in thine arms for briefest season,
Of Germany thou must not ask me,
I cannot bear it there is a reason!
Leave Germany in peace, I do beseech thee,
Vex not with endless questions my poor spirit
Concerning home, friends, social, kind relations,
There is a reason why I cannot bear it.
The oak-tree there is green, the German women
Have soft blue eyes tender they are and fair.
They whisper sighs of hope and truth and passion.
I have good cause 'tis more than I can bear.

VIII.

Whilst I, after other people's,
Others people's darlings gaze,

And before strange sweethearts' dwellings
Sighing pace through weary days.
Then perhaps those other people
In another quarter pine,
Pacing by my very windows,
Coveting that girl of mine.
That were human! God in heaven,
Watch us still whate'er befall!
God in heaven, joy and blessing,
Joy and blessing send us all!

IX.

Dismiss me not, e'en if my thirst
Quenched with that sweet draught be!
Bear with me for a season yet,
That shall suffice for me.
Canst thou no longer be my love,
Then be to me a friend;
For friendship only just begins
When love is at an end.

X.

This mad carnival of loving,
This our heart's intoxication
Ends at last, and we twain, sobered,
Yawningly look each on each.
All the luscious cup is drained
That was filled with sensuous juices,
Foaming to the brim, enticing,
All the luscious cup is drained.
And the violins are silent,
That so sweetly played for dancing,
For the giddy dance of passion
Yes, the violins are silent.
And the lanterns are extinguished,
That with gorgeous light illumined
All the motley troop of maskers
Yes, the lanterns are extinguished.
And to-morrow comes Ash-Wednesday,
I will draw upon thy forehead
Then an ashen cross, and murmur,

Woman, thou art dust remember!

SPRING FESTIVAL

This is the spring-tide's mournful feast,
The frantic troops of blooming girls
Are rushing hither with flying curls,
Moaning they smite their bare white breast,
Adonis! Adonis!
The night has come. By the torches' gleams
They search the forest on every side,
That echoes with anguish far and wide,
With tears, mad laughter, and sobs and screams,
Adonis! Adonis!
The mortal youth so strangely fair,
Lies on the cold turf pale and dead;
His heart's blood staineth the flowers red,
And a wild lament fulfills the air,
Adonis! Adonis!

CHILDE HAROLD

Lo, a large black-shrouded barge
Sadly moves with sails outspread,
And mute creatures' muffled features
Hold grim watch above the dead.
Calm below it lies the poet
With his fair face bare and white,
Still with yearning ever turning
Azure eyes towards heaven's light.
As he saileth sadly waileth
Some bereaven undine-bride.
O'er the springing waves outringing,
Hark! a dirge floats far and wide.

THE ASRA

Daily the fair Sultan's daughter
Wanders to and fro at twilight
By the margin of the fountain,
Where the waters white are rippling.
Daily the young slave at twilight
Stands beside the fountain's margin,
Where the waters white are rippling,
Daily grows he pale and paler.
There one evening moved the princess
Toward the slave with words swift-spoken
"Tell me, tell me what thy name is,
Where thy home is, what thy lineage?"
Spake the youthful slave: "My name is
Mahomet, I come from Yemen;
And by birth I am an Asra,
One who dieth when he loves."

HELENA

Thou hast invoked me from my grave,
And through thy magic spell
Hast quickened me with fierce desire,
This flame thou canst not quell.
Oh press thy lips against my lips,
Divine is mortal breath;
I drink thy very soul from thee.
Insatiable is death.

SONG

There stands a lonely pine-tree
In the north, on a barren height;
He sleeps while the ice and snow flakes
Swathe him in folds of white.
He dreameth of a palm-tree
Far in the sunrise-land,
Lonely and silent longing
On her burning bank of sand.

THE NORTH SEA 1825 TO 1826

TO FREDERICK MERCKEL, THE PICTURES OF THE NORTH SEA
ARE AFFECTIONATELY DEDICATED BY THE AUTHOR.

FIRST CYCLUS

"To be disinterested in everything, but above all in love and friendship, was my supreme wish, my maxim, my practice; hence my daring expression at a later period: 'If I love thee, what is that to thee?' sprang directly from my heart."
Goethe's "Truth and Poetry," Book XIV.

I. CORONATION.

Oh songs of mine! belovèd songs of mine,
Up, up! and don your armor,
And let the trumpets blare,
And lift upon your shield
This youthful maiden
Who now shall reign supreme
Over my heart, as queen!
Hail! hail! thou youthful queen!
From the sun above
I snatch the beaming red gold,
And weave therewith a diadem
For thy consecrated head.
From the fluttering azure-silken canopy of heaven,
Where blaze the diamonds of night,
A precious fragment I cut:
And as a coronation mantle,
I hang it upon thy royal shoulders.
I bestow on thee a court
Of richly-attired sonnets,

Haughty Terzine and stately stanzas.
My wit shall serve thee as courier,
My fancy shall be thy fool,
Thy herald, whose crest is a smiling tear,
Shall be my humor.
But I myself, oh Queen,
Low do I kneel before thee,
On the cushion of crimson samite,
And as homage I dedicate to thee.
The tiny morsel of reason,
That has been compassionately spared me
By thy predecessor in the realm.

II. TWILIGHT.

On the wan shore of the sea
Lonely I sat with troubled thoughts.
The sun dropped lower, and cast
Glowing red streaks on the water.
And the white wide waves,
Crowding in with the tide,
Foamed and rustled, nearer and nearer,
With a strange rustling, a whispering, a hissing,
A laughter, a murmur, a sighing, a seething,
And amidst all these a mysterious lullaby.
I seemed to hear long-past traditions,
Lovely old-time fairy-tales,
Which as a boy I had heard,
From the neighbor's children,
When on summer evenings we had nestled
On the stone steps of the porch.
With little eager hearts,
And wistful cunning eyes,
Whilst the grown maidens
Sat opposite at their windows
Near their sweet-smelling flower pots,
With their rosy faces,
Smiling and beaming in the moonlight.

III. SUNSET.

The glowing red sun descends
Into the wide, tremulous

Silver-gray ocean.
Ethereal, rosy tinted forms
Are wreathed behind him, and opposite,
Through the veil of autumnal, twilight clouds,
Like a sad, deathly-pale countenance,
Breaks the moon,
And after her, like sparks of light,
In the misty distance, shimmer the stars.
Once there shone forth in heaven,
Nuptially united.
Luna the goddess, and Sol the god.
And around them gathered the stars,
Those innocent little children.
But evil tongues whispered dissension,
And in bitterness parted
The lofty, illustrious pair.
Now all day in lonely splendor
The sun-god fares overhead,
Worshiped and magnified in song,
For the excellence of his glory,
By haughty prosperity hardened men.
But at night
In heaven wandereth Luna,
The poor mother,
With her orphaned, starry children;
And she shines with a quiet sadness,
And loving maidens and gentle poets
Dedicate to her their tears and their songs
Poor weak Luna! Womanly-natured,
Still doth she love her beautiful consort.
Towards evening pale and trembling,
She peers forth from light clouds,
And sadly gazes after the departing one,
And in her anguish fain would call to him, "Come!
Come! our children are pining for thee!"
But the scornful sun-god,
At the mere sight of his spouse,
Glows in doubly-dyed purple,
With wrath and grief,
And implacably he hastens downward
To the cold waves of his widowed couch.
Thus did evil-whispering tongues
Bring grief and ruin

Even upon the immortal gods.
And the poor gods in heaven above
Painfully wander
Disconsolate on their eternal path,
And cannot die;
And drag with them
The chain of their glittering misery.
But I, the son of man,
The lowly-born, the death-crowned one,
I murmur no more.

IV. NIGHT ON THE SHORE.

Starless and cold is the night,
The sea yawns;
And outstretched flat on his paunch, over the sea,
Lies the uncouth North-wind.
Secretly with a groaning, stifled voice,
Like a peevish, crabbed man in a freak of good humor,
He babbles to the ocean,
And recounts many a mad tale,
Stories of murderous giants,
Quaint old Norwegian Sagas,
And from time to time, with re-echoing laughter,
He howls forth
The conjuration-songs of the Edda,
With Runic proverbs
So mysteriously arrogant, so magically powerful,
That the white children of the sea
High in the air upspring and rejoice,
Intoxicated with insolence.
Meanwhile on the level beach,
Over the wave-wetted sand,
Strides a stranger whose heart
Is still wilder than wind or wave.
Where his feet fall
Sparks are scattered and shells are cracked.
And he wraps himself closer in his gray mantle,
And walks rapidly through the windy night,
Surely guided by a little light,
That kindly and invitingly beams
From the lonely fisherman's hut.
Father and brother are on the sea,

And quite alone in the hut
Bides the fisher's daughter,
The fisher's rarely-beautiful daughter.
She sits on the hearth,
And listens to the cosy auspicious hum
Of the boiling kettle,
And lays crackling fagots upon the fire.
And blows thereon,
Till the flickering red flames
With a magic charm are reflected
On her blooming face.
On her delicate white shoulders
Which so pathetically outpeep
From the coarse gray smock,
And on her little tidy hand
Which gathers more closely the petticoat
About her dainty loins.
But suddenly the door springs wide,
And in steps the nocturnal stranger
His eyes rest with confident love
On the slim, white maiden,
Who stands trembling before him,
Like a frightened lily.
And he flings his mantle to the ground
And laughs and speaks.
"Thou see'st my child! I keep my word.
And I come, and with me, comes
The olden time when the gods of heaven
Descended to the daughters of men,
And embraced the daughters of men,
And begot with them
A race of sceptre-bearing kings,
And heroes, the wonder of the world.
But thou my child, no longer stand amazed
At my divinity.
And I beseech thee, boil me some tea with rum,
For it is cold out doors,
And in such a night-air as this,
Even we, the eternal gods, must freeze.
And we easily catch a divine catarrh,
And an immortal cough."

V. POSEIDON.

The sunbeams played
Upon the wide rolling sea.
Far out on the roadstead glimmered the vessel
That was to bear me home.
But the favoring wind was lacking,
And still quietly I sat on the white down,
By the lonely shore.
And I read the lay of Odysseus,
The old, the eternally-young lay,
From whose billowy-rushing pages
Joyously into me ascended
The breath of the gods,
And the lustrous spring-tide of humanity,
And the blooming skies of Hellas.
My loyal heart faithfully followed
The son of Laertes in his wanderings and vexations,
By his side I sat with troubled soul,
On the hospitable hearth
Where queens were spinning purple.
And I helped him to lie and happily to escape
From the dens of giants and the arms of nymphs.
And I followed him into Cimmerian night,
Into storm and shipwreck,
And with him I suffered unutterable misery.
With a sigh I spake: "Oh, thou cruel Poseidon,
Fearful is thy wrath,
And I myself tremble
For mine own journey home."
Scarce had I uttered the words,
When the sea foamed,
And from the white billows arose
The reed-crowned head of the sea-god.
And disdainfully he cried:
"Have no fear, Poetling!
Not in the least will I imperil
Thy poor little ship.
Neither will I harass thy precious life
With too considerable oscillations.
For thou, Poetling, hast never offended me,
Thou hast not injured a single turret
On the sacred stronghold of Priam.
Not a single little lash hast thou singed

In the eyelid of my son Polyphemus;
And never hast thou been sagely counselled and protected
By the goddess of wisdom, Pallas Athene."
Thus exclaimed Poseidon,
And plunged again into the sea.
And, at his coarse sailor-wit,
Laughed under the water
Amphitrite, the stout fishwoman,
And the stupid daughters of Nereus.

VI. DECLARATION.

Shadowing downward came dusky evening,
Wildly the breakers rolled,
I sat alone upon the shore and gazed
At the white dance of the waves.
And my bosom heaved with the sea,
A deep homesickness yearningly seized my heart
For thee, oh lovely image,
Who surround'st me everywhere,
Who call'st to me everywhere,
Everywhere, everywhere,
In the rushing of the wind, in the dashing of the sea,
And in the sighing of mine own breast.
With a slender reed I wrote upon the sand,
"Agnes, I love thee!"
But the wicked waves came overflowing
That sweet confession,
And blotted it out.
Oh brittle reed! oh swiftly-scattered sand!
Oh flowing waves, I trust you no more!
The heavens grow darker, my heart beats more wildly,
And with a mighty hand, from the Norwegian woods,
I snatch the loftiest fir,
And I plunge it
Into Etna's glowing gulf;
And, with such a fire-steeped giant's pen,
I write on the dusky canopy of heaven,
"Agnes, I love thee!"
Each night hereafter overhead shall blaze
Those eternal letters of flame.
And all future generations of our descendants
Shall joyously read the celestial sign,

"Agnes, I love thee!"

VII. NIGHT IN THE CABIN.

The ocean hath its pearls,
The heaven hath its stars,
But oh, my heart, my heart,
My heart hath its love.
Great are the sea and the heavens,
But greater is my heart.
And fairer than pearls or stars
Glistens and glows my love,
Thou little, youthful maiden,
Come unto my mighty heart.
My heart, and the sea, and the heavens
Are melting away with love.
On the azure vault of heaven,
Where the beauteous stars are shining,
I am fain to press my lips now,
Wildly press midst stormy weeping.
Yonder myriad stars the eyes are
Of my darling, and they twinkle,
And they beckon to me kindly
From the azure vault of heaven.
Towards the azure vault of heaven,
Towards the eyes of my belovèd,
Piously mine arms uplifting,
Thus I supplicate and worship;
Lovely eyes, ye lights of heaven,
Graciously my soul inspire
Let me die and let me win you,
You and all your spacious heavens.
From the eyes of heaven yonder,
Golden sparks fall trembling downward,
Through the night. My soul dilateth,
Filled and overfilled with passion.
Oh ye eyes of heaven yonder,
Weep yourselves to death within me!
Till my spirit overfloweth
With the radiant starry tear drops.
Cradled by the waves of ocean,
And by drowsy thoughts and visions,
Still I lie within the cabin,

In my berth so dark and narrow.
Through the open hatchway yonder,
I can see the stars clear shining.
The belovèd eyes so gentle,
Of my gentle well-belovèd.
The belovèd eyes so gentle
Hold above my head their vigil;
And they glimmer and they beckon
From the azure vault of heaven.
On the azure vault of heaven,
Still I gaze through blessed hours,
Till a white and filmy vapor
Veils from me those eyes belovèd.
Against the wooden wall of the ship
Where my dreaming head reclines,
Break the waves, the wild sea-waves.
They whisper and murmur
Close into mine ear:
"Oh foolish young fellow,
Thine arm is short and the sky is far off,
And the stars are all firmly nailed above
With golden nails.
Vain is thy yearning and vain is thy sighing!
The best thou canst do is to go to sleep."
I dreamed a dream about a strange vast heath,
All overlaid with white and quiet snow.
And I beneath that white snow buried lay,
And slept the cold and lonely sleep of death.
But from the dark and shadowy heavens yonder,
Upon my grave the starry eyes looked down.
Those gentle eyes! Triumphantly they sparkled,
With still serenity, yet full of love.

VIII. STORM.

The tempest is raging.
It lashes the waves,
And the waves foaming and rearing in wrath
Tower on high, and the white mountains of water
Surge as though they were alive,
While the little ship over-climbs them
With laborious haste,
And suddenly plunges down

Into the black, wide-yawning abyss of the tide.
O sea.
Thou mother of beauty, of the foam-engendered one,
Grandmother of love, spare me!
Already scenting death, flutters around me
The white, ghostly sea-mew,
And whets his beak on the mast.
And hungers with glutton-greed for the heart
Which resounds with the glory of thy daughter,
And which the little rogue, thy grandson,
Hath chosen for his play-ground.
In vain are my prayers and entreaties,
My cry dies away in the rushing storm,
In the battle-tumult of the winds.
They roar and whistle and crackle and howl
Like a bedlam of tones.
And amidst them, distinctly I hear
Alluring notes of harps,
Heart-melting, heart-rending,
And I recognize the voice.
Far away on the rocky Scotch coast,
Where the little gray castle juts out
Over the breaking waves,
There at the lofty-arched window
Stands a beautiful suffering woman,
Transparently delicate, and pale as marble.
And she plays on the harp, and she sings,
And the wind stirs her flowing locks,
And wafts her melancholy song
Over the wide, stormy sea.

IX. CALM.

Calm at sea! The sunbeams flicker
Falling on the level water,
And athwart the liquid jewels
Ploughs the ship her emerald furrows.
By the rudder lies the pilot
On his stomach, gently snoring,
Near the mast, the tarry ship-boy
Stoops at work, the sail repairing.
'Neath their smut his cheeks are ruddy,
Hotly flushed, his broad mouth twitches.

Full of sadness are the glances
Of his eyes so large and lovely.
For the captain stands before him,
Raves and scolds and curses: "Rascal!
Little rascal, thou hast robbed me
Of a herring from the barrel."
Calm at sea! above the water
comes a cunning fish out-peeping.
Warms his little head in sunshine,
Merrily his small fins plashing.
But from airy heights, the sea-mew
On the little fish darts downward.
Carrying in his beak his booty
Back he soars into the azure.

X. AN APPARITION IN THE SEA.

I however lay on the edge of the vessel,
And gazed with dreamy eyes
Down into the glass-clear water.
And gazed deeper and deeper,
Deep down into the bottom of the sea.
At first like a twilight mist,
Then gradually more distinctly colored,
Domes of churches and towers arose,
And at last, as clear as sunshine, a whole city,
An antique Netherland city,
Enlivened with people.
Grave men with black mantles,
And white ruffs, and chains of honor,
And long swords and long faces,
Strode over the swarming market-place,
Towards the court-house with its high steps,
Where the stone effigies of emperors
Kept guard with scepter and sword.
Near by, past long rows of houses,
Past casements like polished mirrors,
And pyramidal, clipped lindens,
Wandered, in rustling silks, the young maidens,
With slender forms, and flower-faces
Decently encircled by their black hoods,
And their waving golden hair.
Motley-clad folk in Spanish garb

Strut past and salute each other.
Elderly dames
In brown, old-fashioned attire,
Missal and rosary in hand,
Hasten with tripping steps
Towards the great cathedral,
Drawn thither by the chiming bells,
And by the deep-voiced tones of the organ.
And the far-off chimes smite me also
With mysterious awe.
Insatiable yearning, profound sadness
Steal into my heart,
Into my scarcely-healed heart.
I feel as if its wounds
Were kissed open by belovèd lips,
And began to bleed afresh,
With hot, red drops,
That fall long and slowly,
On an old house below there,
In the deep city of the sea;
On an old high-gabled house,
Sadly deserted by all living creatures,
Save that in the lower window,
Sits a maiden,
Her head resting on her arms,
Like a poor, forsaken child,
And I know thee, thou poor forsaken child.
Deep down, deep as the sea,
Thou hiddest thyself from me,
In a childish freak,
And never couldst rise again.
And thou sat'st a stranger among strangers,
Through long ages,
Whilst I, my soul full of grief,
I sought thee over the whole earth.
Forever I sought thee,
Thou ever-belovèd,
Thou long-lost,
Thou found at last!
I have found thee, and I see once more
Thy sweet face,
The wise, loyal eyes,
The darling smile,

And never again will I leave thee,
And I come down to thee now,
And with wide-stretched arms,
I leap down upon thy breast.
But just at the right moment
The captain seized me by the foot,
And drew me from the edge of the vessel,
And cried with a peevish laugh,
"Doctor, are you possessed by the devil?"

XI. PURIFICATION.

Remain in thy deep sea-home,
Thou insane dream,
Which so many a night
Hast tortured my heart with a counterfeit happiness,
And which now as a vision of the sea
Dost threaten me even in the broad daylight.
Remain there below to all eternity!
And I cast moreover down unto thee
All my sorrows and sins,
And the cap and bells of folly
That have jingled so long upon my head.
And the cold, sleek serpent's skin
Of dissimulation,
Which so long has enwound my soul
My sick soul,
My God-denying, angel-denying
Wretched soul.
Hilli-ho! Hilli-ho! Here comes the breeze.
Up with the sails! They flutter and belly to the wind.
Over the treacherous smooth plain
Hastens the ship
And the emancipated soul rejoices.

XII. PEACE.

High in heaven stood the sun,
Surrounded by white clouds.
The sea was calm;
And I lay musing on the helm of the ship,
Dreamily musing, and, half-awake,
Half asleep, I saw Christ,

The Savior of the world.
In waving white raiment
He strode gigantically tall
Over land and sea.
His head touched heaven,
He spread his hands in benediction
Over land and sea;
And for a heart in his bosom
He bore the sun,
The red fiery sun,
And the red, fiery sun-heart
Showered its beams of grace,
And its pure love-bestowing light,
That illumines and warms
Over land and sea.
Peals of festal bells drew hither and thither,
As swans might draw by chains of roses
The smooth-gliding vessel,
And sportively drew it to the verdant banks,
Where folk dwelt in a lofty-towered
Overhanging town.
Oh miracle of peace! How quiet was the town!
Hushed was the dull murmur of chattering, sweltering Trade.
And through the clean, resounding streets,
Walked people clad in white,
Bearing branches of palm.
And when two such would meet,
They looked at each other with ardent sympathy
And, trembling with love and self denial,
Kissed each other's brow,
And glanced upward
Towards the sun-heart of the Savior,
Which in glad propitiation irradiated downward
Its crimson blood:
And thrice they exclaimed,
"Praised be Jesus Christ!"
Couldst thou have conceived this vision,
What wouldst thou have given,
Most dearly belovèd,
Thou who art so weak in body and mind,
And so strong in faith!
Thou who so singly honorest the Trinity,
Who kissest daily the pug and the reins and the paws

Of thy lofty protectress,
And hastenest with canting devotion
To the Aulic councilor and to the councilor of justice,
And at last to the council of the Realm
In the pious city,
Where sand and faith flourish,
And the long-suffering waters of the sacred Spree
Purify souls and dilute tea.
Couldst thou have conceived this vision
Most dearly belovèd,
Thou hadst borne it to the lofty minnows of the market place,
With thy pale blinking countenance,
Rapt with piety and humility;
And their high mightinesses
Ravished and trembling with ecstacy,
Would have fallen praying with thee on their knees,
And their eyes glowing with beatitude,
Would have promised thee an increase of salary,
Of a hundred thalers Prussian currency.
And thou wouldst have stammered with folded hands,
"Praised be Jesus Christ!"

SECOND CYCLUS

Motto
Xenophon's Anabasis IV. V.

I. SALUTATION TO THE SEA.

Thalatta! Thalatta!
All hail to thee, thou Eternal sea!
All hail to thee ten thousand times
From my jubilant heart,
As once thou wast hailed
By ten thousand Grecian hearts,
Misfortune-combating, homeward-yearning,
World-renowned Grecian hearts.
The waters heaved,
They heaved and roared.
The sun poured streaming downward
Its flickering rosy lights.
The startled flocks of sea-mews
Fluttered away with shrill screams;
The coursers stamped, the shields rattled,
And far out, resounded like a triumphal pæan,
Thalatta! Thalatta!
All hail to thee, thou Eternal Sea!
Like the language of home, thy water whispers to me.
Like the dreams of my childhood I see it glimmer,
Over thy billowy realm of waves.
And it repeats to me anew olden memories,

Of all the belovèd glorious sports,
Of all the twinkling Christmas gifts,
Of all the ruddy coral-trees,
Tiny golden fishes, pearls and bright-hued mussels,
Which thou dost secretly preserve
Below there in thy limpid house of crystal.
Oh, how I have pined in barren exile!
Like a withered flower
In the tin box of a botanist,
My heart lay in my breast.
I feel as if all winter I had sat,
A sick man, in a dark, sick room,
Which now I suddenly leave.
And dazzlingly shines down upon me
The emerald spring, the sunshine-awakened spring,
And the white-blossomed trees are rustling;
And the young flowers look at me,
With their many-colored, fragrant eyes.
And there is an aroma, and a murmuring, and a breathing and a laughter,
And in the blue sky the little birds are singing,
Thalatta! Thalatta!
Thou valiant, retreating heart,
How oft, how bitter oft
Did the fair barbarians of the North press thee hard!
From their large victorious eyes
They darted burning shafts.
With crooked, polished words,
They threatened to cleave my breast.
With sharp-pointed missives they shattered
My poor, stunned brain.
In vain I held up against them my shield,
The arrows whizzed, the strokes cracked,
And from the fair barbarians of the North
I was pressed even unto the sea.
And now with deep, free breath, I hail the sea,
The dear, redeeming sea
Thalatta! Thalatta!

II. TEMPEST.

Gloomy lowers the tempest over the sea,
And through the black wall of cloud
Is unsheathed the jagged lightning,

Swift outflashing, and swift-vanishing,
Like a jest from the brain of Chronos.
Over the barren, billowy water,
Far away rolls the thunder,
And up leap the white water-steeds,
Which Boreas himself begot
Out of the graceful mare of Erichthon,
And the sea-birds flutter around,
Like the shadowy dead on the Styx,
Whom Charon repels from his nocturnal boat.
Poor, merry, little vessel,
Dancing yonder the most wretched of dances!
Eolus sends it his liveliest comrades,
Who wildly play to the jolliest measures;
One pipes his horn, another blows,
A third scrapes his growling bass-viol.
And the uncertain sailor stands at the rudder,
And constantly gazes at the compass,
The trembling soul of the ship;
And he raises his hands in supplication to Heaven
"Oh, save me, Castor, gigantic hero!
And thou conquering wrestler, Pollux."

III. WRECKED.

Hope and love! everything shattered
And I myself, like a corpse
That the growling sea has cast up,
I lie on the strand,
On the barren cold strand.
Before me surges the waste of waters,
Behind me lies naught but grief and misery;
And above me, march the clouds,
The formless, gray daughters of the air,
Who from the sea, in buckets of mist,
Draw the water,
And laboriously drag and drag it,
And spill it again in the sea
A melancholy, tedious task,
And useless as my own life.
The waves murmur, the sea mews scream,
Old recollections possess me;
Forgotten dreams, banished visions,

Tormentingly sweet, uprise.
There lives a woman in the North,
A beautiful woman, royally beautiful.
Her slender, cypress-like form
Is swathed in a light, white raiment.
Her locks, in their dusky fullness,
Like a blessed night,
Streaming from her braid-crowned head,
Curl softly as a dream
Around the sweet, pale face;
And from the sweet pale face
Large and powerful beams an eye,
Like a black sun.
Oh thou black sun, how oft,
How rapturously oft, I drank from thee
The wild flames of inspiration!
And stood and reeled, intoxicated with fire.
Then there hovered a smile as mild as a dove,
About the arched, haughty lips.
And the arched, haughty lips
Breathed forth words as sweet as moonlight,
And delicate as the fragrance of the rose.
And my soul soared aloft,
And flew like an eagle up into the heavens.
Silence ye waves and sea mews!
All is over! joy and hope
Hope and love! I lie on the ground
An empty, shipwrecked man,
And press my glowing face
Into the moist sand.

IV. SUNSET.

The beautiful sun
Has quietly descended into the sea.
The surging water is already tinted
By dusky night
But still the red of evening
Sprinkles it with golden lights.
And the rushing might of the tide
Presses toward the shore the white waves,
That merrily and nimbly leap
Like woolly flocks of sheep,

Which at evening the singing shepherd boy
Drives homeward.
"How beautiful is the sun!"
Thus spake after a long silence, the friend
Who wandered with me on the beach.
And, half in jest, half in sober sadness,
He assured me that the sun
Was a beautiful woman, who had for policy
Espoused the old god of the sea.
All day she wanders joyously
In the lofty heavens, decked with purple,
And sparkling with diamonds;
Universally beloved, universally admired
By all creatures of the globe,
And cheering all creatures of the globe
With the radiance and warmth of her glance.
But at evening, wretchedly constrained,
She returns once more
To the wet home, to the empty arms
Of her hoary spouse.
"Believe me," added my friend,
And laughed and sighed, and laughed again,
"They live down there in the daintiest wedlock;
Either they sleep or else they quarrel,
Until high upheaves the sea above them,
And the sailor amidst the roaring of the waves can hear
How the old fellow berates his wife:
'Round strumpet of the universe!
Sunbeam coquette!
The whole day you shine for others,
And at night for me you are frosty and tired.'
After such curtain lectures,
Quite naturally bursts into tears
The proud sun, and bemoans her misery,
And bemoans so lamentably long, that the sea god
Suddenly springs desperately out of his bed,
And quickly swims up to the surface of the ocean,
To collect his wits and to breathe."
Thus did I myself see him yester-night,
Uprise from the bosom of the sea.
He had a jacket of yellow flannel,
And a lily-white night cap,
And a withered countenance.

V. THE SONG OF THE OCEANIDES.

'Tis nightfall and paler grows the sea.
And alone with his lonely soul,
There sits a man on the cold strand
And turns his death-cold glances
Towards the vast, death-cold vault of heaven,
And toward the vast, billowy sea.
On airy sails float forth his sighs;
And melancholy they return,
And find the heart close-locked,
Wherein they fain would anchor.
And he groans so loud that the white sea-mews,
Startled out of their sandy nests,
Flutter circling around him.
And he laughingly speaks to them thus:
"Ye black-legged birds,
With white wings, oversea flutterers!
With crooked beaks, salt-water bibbers,
Ye oily seal-flesh devourers!
Your life is as bitter as your food.
I, however, the fortunate, taste naught but sweets!
I taste the fragrance of the rose,
The moonshine-nourished bride of the nightingale.
I taste still sweeter sugar-plums,
Stuffed with whipped cream.
And the sweetest of all things I taste,
The sweets of loving and of being loved!
"She loves me, she loves me, the dear girl!
Now stands she at home on the balcony of her house,
And gazes forth in the twilight upon the street,
And listens and yearns for me, really!
Vainly does she glance around, and sigh,
And sighing she descends to the garden,
And wanders midst the fragrance and the moonlight,
And talks to the flowers, and tells them
How I, her belovèd, am so lovely and so lovable really!
Later in her bed, in her sleep, in her dreams,
Blissfully she hovers about my precious image,
So that in the morning at breakfast
Upon the glistening buttered bread,
She sees my smiling face,

And she devours it for sheer love really!"
Thus boasted and boasted he,
And meanwhile screamed the sea-mews,
As with cold, ironical tittering.
The twilight mists ascended,
Uncannily forth from lilac clouds
Peered the greenish-yellow moon.
Loud roared the billows,
And deep from the loud roaring sea,
As plaintive as a whispering monsoon,
Sounded the song of the Oceanides
Of the beautiful, compassionate mermaids,
Distinct midst them all the lovely voice
Of the silver-footed spouse of Peleus
And they sigh and sing:
"Oh fool, thou fool, thou boasting fool,
Tormented with misery!
Destroyed are all thy hopes,
The playful children of the heart
And ah! thy heart, Niobe-like,
Is petrified with grief!
In thy brain falls the night,
And therein are unsheathed the lightnings of frenzy,
And thou makest a boast of thy trouble!
Oh fool, thou fool, thou boasting fool!
Stiff-necked art thou as thy forefather,
The lofty Titan, who stole celestial fire
From the gods, and bestowed it upon man.
And tortured by eagles chained to the rock,
Olympus-high he flung defiance, flung defiance and groaned,
Till we heard it in the depths of the sea,
And came to him with the song of consolation.
Oh fool, thou fool, thou boasting fool!
Thou, however, art more impotent still.
'Twere more seemly that thou shouldst honor the gods,
And patiently bear the burden of misery,
And patiently bear it, long, so long,
Till Atlas himself would lose patience,
And cast from his shoulders the ponderous world
Into eternal night."
So rang the song of the Oceanides,
Of the beautiful compassionate mermaids,
Until louder waves overpowered it.

Behind the clouds retired the moon,
The night yawned,
And I sat long thereafter in the darkness and wept.

VI. THE GODS OF GREECE.

Full-blooming moon, in thy radiance,
Like flowing gold shines the sea.
With daylight clearness, yet twilight enchantment,
Thy beams lie over the wide, level beach.
And in the pure, blue starless heavens,
Float the white clouds,
Like colossal images of gods
Of gleaming marble.
No more again! those are no clouds!
They are themselves the gods of Hellas,
Who erst so joyously governed the world,
But now, supplanted and dead,
Yonder, like monstrous ghosts, must fare,
Through the midnight skies.
Amazed and strangely dazzled, I contemplate
The ethereal Pantheon.
The solemnly mute, awfully agitated,
Gigantic forms.
There is Chronos yonder, the king of heaven;
Snow-white are the curls of his head,
The world-renowned Olympus-shaking curls.
He holds in his hand the quenched lightning,
In his face dwell misfortune and grief;
But even yet the olden pride.
Those were better days, oh Zeus,
When thou didst celestially divert thyself
With youths and nymphs and hecatombs.
But the gods themselves, reign not forever;
The young supplant the old,
As thou thyself, thy hoary father,
And thy Titan-uncle didst supplant
Jupiter-Parricida!
Thee also, I recognize, haughty Juno;
Despite all thy jealous care,
Another has wrested thy sceptre from thee,
And thou art no longer Queen of Heaven.
And thy great eyes are blank,

And thy lily arms are powerless,
And nevermore may thy vengeance smite
The divinely-quickened Virgin,
And the miracle-performing son of God.
Thee also I recognize, Pallas Athena!
With thy shield and thy wisdom, could'st thou not avert
The ruin of the gods?
Also thee I recognize, thee also, Aphrodite!
Once the golden, now the silvern!
'Tis true that the love-charmed zone still adorns thee
But I shudder with horror at thy beauty.
And if thy gracious body were to favor me
Like other heroes, I should die of terror.
Thou seemest to me a goddess-corpse,
Venus Libitina!
No longer glances toward thee with love,
Yonder the dread Ares!
How melancholy looks Phoebus Apollo
The youth. His lyre is silent,
Which once so joyously resounded at the feast of the gods.
Still sadder looks Hephaistos.
And indeed nevermore shall the limper
Stumble into the service of Hebe,
And nimbly pour forth to the assemblage
The luscious nectar. And long ago was extinguished
The unextinguishable laughter of the gods.
I have never loved you, ye gods!
For to me are the Greeks antipathetic,
And even the Romans are hateful.
But holy compassion and sacred pity
Penetrate my heart,
When I now gaze upon you yonder,
Deserted gods!
Dead night-wandering shadows,
Weak as mists which the wind scares away.
And when I recall how dastardly and visionary
Are the gods who have supplanted you,
The new, reigning, dolorous gods,
Mischief-plotters in the sheep's clothing of humility,
Oh then a more sullen rancor possesses me,
And I fain would shatter the new Temples,
And battle for you, ye ancient gods,
For you and your good ambrosial cause.

And before your high altars,
Rebuilt with their extinguished fires,
Fain would I kneel and pray,
And supplicating uplift mine arms.
Always ye ancient gods,
Even in the battles of mortals,
Always did ye espouse the cause of the victor.
But man is more magnanimous than ye,
And in the battles of the gods, he now takes the part
Of the gods who have been vanquished.
Thus spake I, and lo, visibly blushed
Yonder the wan cloud figures,
And they gazed upon me like the dying,
Transfigured by sorrow, and suddenly disappeared.
The moon was concealed
Behind dark advancing clouds.
Loud roared the sea.
And triumphantly came forth in the heavens
The eternal stars.

VII. THE PHŒNIX.

A bird comes flying out of the West;
He flies to the Eastward,
Towards the Eastern garden-home,
Where spices shed fragrance, and flourish,
And palms rustle and fountains scatter coolness.
And in his flight the magic bird sings:
"She loves him! she loves him!
She carries his portrait in her little heart,
And she carries it sweetly and secretly hidden,
And knoweth it not herself!
But in dreams he stands before her.
She implores and weeps and kisses his hands,
And calls his name,
And calling she awakes, and she lies in affright,
And amazed she rubs her beautiful eyes,
She loves him! she loves him!"
Leaning on the mast on the upper deck,
I stood and heard the bird's song.
Like blackish-green steeds with silver manes,
Leapt the white crisp-curling waves.
Like flocks of swans glided past,

With gleaming sails, the Helgolands,
The bold nomads of the North Sea.
Above me in the eternal blue
Fluttered white clouds,
And sparkled the eternal sun,
The Rose of heaven, the fire-blossoming,
Which joyously was mirrored in the sea.
And the heavens and seas and mine own heart
Resounded in echo
She loves him! she loves him!

VIII. QUESTION.

By the sea, by the desolate nocturnal sea,
Stands a youthful man,
His breast full of sadness, his head full of doubt.
And with bitter lips he questions the waves:
"Oh solve me the riddle of life!
The cruel, world-old riddle,
Concerning which, already many a head hath been racked.
Heads in hieroglyphic-hats,
Heads in turbans and in black caps,
Periwigged heads, and a thousand other
Poor, sweating human heads.
Tell me, what signifies man?
Whence does he come? whither does he go?
Who dwells yonder above the golden stars?"
The waves murmur their eternal murmur,
The winds blow, the clouds flow past.
Cold and indifferent twinkle the stars,
And a fool awaits an answer.

IX. SEA-SICKNESS.

The gray afternoon clouds
Drop lower over the sea,
Which darkly riseth to meet them,
And between them both fares the ship.
Sea-sick I still sit by the mast
And all by myself indulge in meditation,
Those world-old ashen-gray meditations,
Which erst our father Lot entertained,
When he had enjoyed too much of a good thing,

And afterward suffered such inconvenience.
Meanwhile I think also of old stories;
How pilgrims with the cross on their breast in days of yore,
On their stormy voyages, devoutly kissed
The consoling image of the blessed Virgin.
How sick knights in such ocean-trials,
Pressed to their lips with equal comfort
The dear glove of their lady.
But I sit and chew in vexation
An old herring, my salty comforter,
Midst caterwauling and dogged tribulation.
Meanwhile the ship wrestles
With the wild billowy tide.
Like a rearing war-horse she stands erect,
Upon her stern, till the helm cracks.
Now crashes she headforemost downward once more
Into the howling abyss of waters,
Then again, as if recklessly love-languid,
She tries to recline
On the black bosom of the gigantic waves,
Which powerfully seethe upward,
And immediately a chaotic ocean-cataract
Plunges down in crisp-curling whiteness,
And covers me with foam.
This shaking and swinging and tossing
Is unendurable!
Vainly mine eye peers forth and seeks
The German coast. But alas! only water,
And everywhere water turbulent water!
Even as the traveller in winter, thirsts
For a warm cordial cup of tea,
So does my heart now thirst for thee
My German fatherland.
May thy sweet soil ever be covered
With lunacy, hussars and bad verses,
And thin, lukewarm treatises.
May thy zebras ever be fattened
On roses instead of thistles.
Ever may thy noble apes
Haughtily strut in negligent attire,
And esteem themselves better than all other
Priggish heavy-footed, horned cattle.
May thine assemblies of snails

Ever deem themselves immortal
Because they crawl forward so slowly;
And may they daily convoke in full force,
To discuss whether the cheesemould belongs to the cheese;
And still longer may they convene
To decide how best to honor the Egyptian sheep,
So that its wool may improve
And it may be shorn like others,
With no difference.
Forever may folly and wrong
Cover thee all over, oh Germany,
Nevertheless I yearn towards thee
For at least thou art dry land.

X. IN PORT.

Happy the man who has reached port,
And left behind the sea and the tempest,
And who now sits, quietly and warm,
In the goodly town-cellar of Bremen.
How pleasantly and cordially
The world is mirrored in the wine-glass.
And how the waving microcosm
Pours sunnily down into the thirsty heart!
I see everything in the glass,
Ancient and modern tribes,
Turks and Greeks, Hegel and Gans,
Citron groves and guard-parades,
Berlin and Schilda, and Tunis and Hamburg.
Above all the image of my belovèd,
The little angel-head against the golden background of Rhine-wine.
Oh how beautiful! how beautiful thou art, belovèd!
Thou art like a rose.
Not like the Rose of Shiraz,
The Hafiz-besung bride of the nightingale.
Not like the Rose of Sharon,
The sacred purple extolled by the prophet.
Thou art like the rose in the wine-cellar of Bremen.
That is the rose of roses,
The older it grows the fairer it blooms,
And its celestial perfume has inspired me.
And did not mine host of the town-cellar of Bremen
Hold me fast, fast by my hair,

I should tumble head over heels.
The worthy man! we sat together,
And drank like brothers.
We spake of lofty, mysterious things,
We sighed and sank in each other's arms.
And he led me back to the religion of love:
I drank to the health of my bitterest enemy,
And I forgave all bad poets,
As I shall some day hope to be forgiven myself.
I wept with fervor of piety, and at last
The portals of salvation were opened to me,
Where the twelve Apostles, the holy wine-butts,
Preach in silence and yet so intelligibly
Unto all people.
Those are men!
Without, unseemly in their wooden garb,
Within, they are more beautiful and brilliant
Than all the haughty Levites of the Temple,
And the guards and courtiers of Herod,
Decked with gold and arrayed in purple.
But I have always averred
That not amidst quite common folk
No, in the very best society,
Perpetually abides the King of Heaven.
Hallelujah! How lovely around me
Wave the palms of Beth-El!
How fragrant are the myrrh-trees of Hebron!
How the Jordan rustles and reels with joy!
And my immortal soul also reels,
And I reel with her, and, reeling,
The worthy host of the town-cellar of Bremen
Leads me up-stairs into the light of day.
Thou worthy host of the town-cellar of Bremen,
Seest thou on the roofs of the houses,
Sit the angels, and they are drunk and they sing.
The glowing sun up yonder
Is naught but a red drunken nose.
The nose of the spirit of the universe,
And around the red nose of the spirit of the universe
Reels the whole tipsy world.

XI. EPILOGUE

Like the stalks of wheat in the fields,
So flourish and wave in the mind of man
His thoughts.
But the delicate fancies of love
Are like gay little intermingled blossoms
Of red and blue flowers.
Red and blue flowers!
The surly reaper rejects you as useless.
The wooden flail scornfully thrashes you,
Even the luckless traveler,
Whom your aspect delights and refreshes,
Shakes his head,
And calls you beautiful weeds.
But the rustic maiden,
The wearer of garlands,
Honors you, and plucks you,
And adorns with you her fair locks.
And thus decorated she hastens to the dancing-green
Where the flutes and fiddles sweetly resound;
Or to the quiet bushes
Where the voice of her beloved soundeth sweeter still
Than fiddles or flutes.

Printed in Great Britain
by Amazon